What People Are Saying About

The Wool Ball, the Smelly Cat and the Cranky Corpse

With his keen ethnographic mind, the author revealingly examines his profound dreams and synchronicities. His many deep analyses demonstrate that active engagement awakens deep psychological and spiritual growth.
Bernard Beitman, MD, Founder and President of the Coincidence Project

The author uncovers the mystery of human experience by sharing his personal and poignant stories. As a social scientist fascinated by ethnographic research on vulnerable groups, he delves into his own struggles with anxiety and fear, loss and grief, and the illness of his daughter. Through painting, dreams, meditation, and narratives we are invited on a journey of enlightenment and recovery with, at the same time, a glance at synchronicity and coincidence. This is a courageous project embracing all ways of knowing in his writing about intricate relationships with the self, family, friends and nature.
Eddie Chiu, PhD, clinical psychologist and professor at Alliant International University

This beautiful book conveys a view of the world in which our living is vividly interpenetrated by a second life of dreams and synchronicities. The author writes with intelligence, grace and insight. His words are like a path. A path to the edge of mystery. Where you meet, not only his heart, but your own.
Rob Foxcroft, author of *Feeling Hear*

This book is a profound revelation of reality as an intricate multi-layered complexity where sensing, dream symbols and implicit knowing are available to be formulated into a new understanding of life. We re-experience our own reality in order to make sense of it, as well as re-experience others' experiences to understand theirs—just as readers re-experience and dip into the intriguing reality articulated in this book.
Akira Ikemi, PhD, Professor, Kansai University

The Wool Ball, the Smelly Cat and the Cranky Corpse

Awakening to Coincidences

The Wool Ball, the Smelly Cat and the Cranky Corpse

Awakening to Coincidences

Manny Mak

MANTRA BOOKS

London, UK
Washington, DC, USA

CollectiveInk

First published by Mantra Books, 2025
Mantra Books is an imprint of Collective Ink Ltd.,
Unit 11, Shepperton House, 89 Shepperton Road, London, N1 3DF
office@collectiveinkbooks.com
www.collectiveinkbooks.com
www.mantra-books.net

For distributor details and how to order please visit the 'Ordering' section on our website.

ISBN: 978 1 80341 955 8
978 1 80341 957 2 (ebook)
Library of Congress Control Number: 2024918890

A CIP catalogue record for this book is available from the British Library.

Design: Lapiz Digital Services

UK: Printed and bound by CPI Group (UK) Ltd, Croydon, CR0 4YY
Printed in North America by CPI GPS partners

We operate a distinctive and ethical publishing philosophy in all areas of our business, from our global network of authors to production and worldwide distribution.

A True Fable

dreams play out in waking life
like a fable
slowly unveiling from the depths
a flower blossoms
thirty stamens whisper in kaleidoscopic silence
in ruins and rubble
softly sung hymns can be heard from afar

This book contains mention of suicidal ideation, mental health disorders, eating disorders, and animal injury. Reader discretion is advised

Contents

Foreword

by Rob Foxcroft, author of Feeling Heard, Hearing Others

Reading this beautiful book as somebody with a European cultural background, I found myself thinking of Jung's *Memories, Dreams and Reflections* and *The Red Book*. I remembered some of the visionary writings of Laurens van der Post and I thought of the deep healing which took place during the making of Alice Miller's *Pictures of a Childhood*.

As you read this book, you are drawn into a fascinating and distinctive view of the world, in which our living is vividly interpenetrated by a second life of dreams and synchronicities. You cannot fail to be charmed by the sense that you are meeting a lovely human being at a most intimate level, nor could you fail to be aware of his intelligence, grace and insight.

The story reads like a thriller – a poetic thriller with the mysteries of an unseen world always unfolding within it. You are anxious for the author's daughter as she wrestles with the uncertain outcome of a serious eating disorder. You are haunted by the threat of imprisonment hanging over the storyteller. You fear with him the shadows of dangerous men.

The prose is never less than captivating and the story is illuminated by a series of exquisite paintings so that, in the end, I was reminded above all of the great poet-painter, Wang Wei, in the synthesis of words and images.

In a Chinese painting of 'mountains-and-waters', there is always a winding path. The path leads to a threshold. And everything leads inwards to the heart. In this life-enhancing book, there are these same elements. The words are like a path. A path to the edge of mystery. Where you meet, not only the author's heart, but your own.

Acknowledgments

I would like to express my heartfelt thanks to Joyce Foxcroft, who carefully edited the manuscript to make it presentable and fit for publication; and to Rob Foxcroft, who subtly crafted his succinct, empathetic and inviting Foreword. Special thanks to Olivia for coming up with a fresh new title for the book.

I am very grateful to all the friends from the Focusing Institute, the Dream Workshop, Fountain Retreat, and Seraphim Fellowship, for their support and encouragement in difficult times.

Finally, to my lovely wife and talented daughter, I treasure your love, support, and company. We have sailed through challenges bigger than we thought we could handle. We survive; we have each other. Love you always.

Prologue: The Beginning of a Spiritual Journey

My daughter woke me up, softly whispering words I could barely hear, but using exaggerated facial expressions I could hardly ignore, "Two men are here asking for you."

Standing at the door were two heavily built men in black suits. They didn't come in. They were private investigators hired by a big financial corporation. One showed me his card, the other handed me a legal document. "Ask your lawyers to follow up," he uttered sternly, without further elaboration.

I read the document. It asked for the monetary transaction records of a corporate social responsibility (CSR) initiative of which I am a director. The parent company of the CSR initiative was involved in high-risk investments incurring colossal debts. As I read the details, my heart sank, but I didn't experience any anxiety. I signed, and they left.

For the moment I was calm. I had no fear, but it surfaced little by little afterward, growing to slow-burning anxiety and then to throat-choking dread when the lawyers explained that I could be facing grave legal and financial consequences. It was in the middle of the prolonged crisis of the Covid-19 pandemic. The unpredictability of the rapidly changing social circumstances at that time fed into the ordeal and made it worse.

My regular weekly hike with a group of retired friends was scheduled that morning. I didn't skip it. I joined the group on time. The hike had resumed after stopping for a few months because of several Covid outbreaks in the community. Fellow hikers were delighted to see each other. I mingled, smiled, and chatted as if nothing had happened. In fact, in the following months, only a few of my friends ever learned of my situation. People are wary of the risk of the unknown. Better be discreet.

Walking along the hiking trails, mind blank, my heart was saddened, filled with the weight of a bag of stones. But hiking in the countryside was much better than fretting at home and pondering restlessly on the things to come.

It had started to rain when we arrived at a difficult climb. A few hikers had gone up but the remainder waited for the rain to stop. The hill was a dozen meters high and too slippery under the pouring rain. After a long wait and a few failed attempts, we decided to go for another, less difficult trail. No good working against the weather. One fellow hiker jokingly said, "If Mother Nature warns you time and again, give in. Don't argue!"

The rain and the detour kept my mind occupied. It was good. I didn't have time to think. But as the sky cleared, the thorny events to come kept pressing on me. The phone rang. A meeting with the lawyers was set up for the afternoon. There are two of us involved in the case. Brian and I are directors of the charitable initiative, which is a subsidiary company, a small division of the CSR taking care of social services, with the executives and founders of the parent investment company shouldering major liability.

As the group rested by a small reservoir, I decided to cancel my lectures and talks in the coming months. I sent out a few brief text messages. The disappointed organizers were curious and questioning, but I didn't allow myself to give the slightest hint of what was going on.

This is just a snapshot of the commotion that has been going on since that morning. What happened to me has been hectic and eventful, but the events inside me have been much more significant and long-lasting. Amid the emotional turmoil came a series of coincidences, which turned enigmas into meanings, sufferings into blessings, and life-long egoic pursuits into compassionate redemption. I have experienced synchronicities in dreams and in my waking life. So has my daughter, who suffers from a life-threatening eating disorder. She wrestles with her inner demons -- a messy wool ball, a smelly cat and a cranky corpse, imagined and real, ethereal but deeply entwined with her life. This book is a diary of my endeavor to understand the coincidences I have experienced, to stay with my daughter on her long road of recovery, and to find a spiritual anchor for this earthly life.

Each chapter begins with a painting that drawn in a mindful and meditative state. It is a visual account of the chapter that follows. Throughout the book, names, places, personal particulars and the specifics of events have been altered and obscured for anonymity, but I have documented dreams and visions as accurately as I can. Among them, the most pivotal is the dream which carries the archetypal symbol of a sacrificial lamb. In the timespan of two years, the dream has gradually unfolded its meaning: it is an invitation for me to give a peace offering for myself, my family, and for K-Town, the city I reside in. The journey began at midnight on March 23, 2021.

Chapter 1

Meditative Focusing and the Dragon Dream

A Midnight Call

It all began at midnight on March 23, 2021, when I received a phone call inviting me to participate in a CSR initiative to provide psychiatric support for citizens of K-Town, especially those afflicted by the pandemic. K-Town is a multi-ethnic city with a significant proportion of the population of Hakka Chinese descent.

It was quite a peculiar situation when my phone rang. I was waiting for my daughter, Constance, to get off from work. Despite taking anti-anxiety drugs, she was still anxious about her diet. She had a severe eating disorder. A rule allowed no eating after 8:00 pm, and her panic attack would be unrelenting if she couldn't get back home for dinner before this deadline. For the past few years, I had given her a ride home almost every workday to help tame her anxiety.

That evening, I waited for six hours before finally getting her in the car at 2:00 am. The street was empty. She was abysmally beaten, teetering on the brink of collapse. Part of her eating disorder meant that she couldn't voice her needs, especially to her superior at work. Despite the boiling emotions inside her, she had held tight to her calm composure and stayed in her office for hours. She didn't eat. She could have asked for a short dinner break or a time out for a walk as she was only on standby to help her boss revise an urgent proposal. But she didn't make any request, just sat there, frozen. I didn't want to add any extra straw to her back, so I told her I was fine waiting, working on my column in a small basketball court nearby. I texted her, "Don't worry about me, I am drafting my essay. You need your father to stand by your side."

A well-known medical doctor phoned me and explained that the charitable endeavor was reliable. The parent investment company laid aside a small but regular percentage of its revenue to finance the CSR operations. Providing free psychiatric care for the public was a long-term commitment. The financial implications were huge, and so was the workload I might have to shoulder. When the conversation ended, I strolled back and forth in the empty courtyard. I had worries. As my daughter was very much dependent on my support, it would be detrimental to her if I got myself entangled in some demanding operations. I ought to decline the invitation to become involved.

But the other side of me argued with compelling force. Supporting those suffering from psychological trauma has been a serious undertaking dear to my heart and I have written a lot about my commitment to this. If I declined I would be going against my own conviction and belief. At that very moment, the column I was drafting was encouraging readers to care about each other's wellbeing in challenging times. After some soul searching, I agreed to attend a briefing the following day.

As I recall the sequence of events, the very beginning of this prolonged legal entanglement – that ground zero at the basketball court – was a meaningful coincidence that I wasn't aware of until months later. That was the only time I had had such a long wait for my distressed daughter, long into the night. Amid her agony, she texted me from inside the restroom of her office, in tears. She was screaming inside, but she couldn't make the slightest squawk.

Scrolling back to the text messages I wrote her on that night, I read, "Mother Nature is generous. Sunshine is for everyone. All you have to do is face the light."

On my mind as I wrote the text to my daughter was an obscure poem she used to cite. It is recited in a scene at the very end of the last episode of the TV mini-series *11.22.63*, an adaptation of Stephen King's book of the same title.

We did not ask for this room,
or this music;
we were invited in.
Therefore,
because the dark surrounds us,
let us turn our faces toward the light.
Let us endure hardship
to be grateful for plenty.
We have been given pain
to be astounded by joy.
We have been given life
to deny death.
We did not ask for this room,
or this music.
But because we are here,
let us dance.

Her reading of this poem was quite different from mine. She had a burning sensation when she read "let us turn our faces toward the light," as if she was scorched by the imaginary heat. While for me this line reminds me of the bible verses, "The Word gave life to everything that was created, and his life brought light to everyone. The light shines in the darkness, and the darkness can never extinguish it."

I encouraged her to step into the bright side of life. But later, when I looked at things through her eyes, I could vicariously share her feeling of cuddling down in darkness and fearing the scorching sun. It seemed an unfathomable paradox that the inertia of her depression made her feel safe, even when she was in the darkness of pain and hardship. It is easy for us to say, "Face the light, and light will effortlessly extinguish darkness." But for those who are deep in their sufferings, a leap of faith is difficult. She used to say the poem struck a chord in her. There were some contradictory emotions she couldn't understand. At that time, to be astounded by joy was still far off.

Looking back, my daughter's recovery has been inexplicably intertwined with the events that unfolded after that midnight call. My predicament, unknown to me at that time, has speeded up my psychological and spiritual growth, and in turn, my experience has inspired my daughter to sail through life challenges of her own.

Focusing

Ten years ago, in my early 50s, I had a pretty good career in academia, a good marriage, and a lovely daughter working diligently at the beginning of her career. In the eyes of my relatives, friends, colleagues, and students, I was living a good life. I thought so too, for I had been working extremely hard to be a good husband, a liberal father, an innovative researcher, and a caring teacher. But I was gradually running out of steam, like an orange which looks normal from the outside but is drying up inside.

I had a tough time maintaining my stamina. Not that I was not performing, but as my research grants got bigger, my projects lost the novelty they used to have.

My wife, Teresa, had a successful career as a physical therapist. We were both content with a family life that was peaceful, but our hearts and minds were drifting apart as the years went by. So was my daughter. She had a good relationship with us, but all three of us lived separate lives. Teresa and I were not aware of Constance's depression until a late stage. The irony was that I was not aware of my own depression either.

Like Constance, I was able to perform very well despite my depression. No one sensed any problem in me, not even myself. I was as energetic as a stand-up comedian when I was lecturing, immediately switching off when I left the lecture hall. I ate my lunch alone. I didn't answer the knock on my office door. I drank a lot before going to bed, but I wouldn't go over the tipping point of being drunk. This had been going on for many years, until I finally decided to retire early and mend the broken shards of my shattered life.

There are many roads to the inner journey of our earthly life: prayer, meditation, yoga, mainstream, and alternative therapies... When one's life is leading toward a dead end, I believe a door will be opened for the willing soul.

Eugene Gendlin, the late philosopher and psychologist at the University of Chicago, initiator of a practice called "Focusing", was a door opened for me. He analyzed thousands of therapist-patient sessions recorded on tape and found that successful cases were those in which the clients talked differently and had a willingness to change. They made successful changes because they did something inside themselves, irrespective of the therapists' techniques – "differences in methods of therapy seem to mean surprisingly little." Gendlin turned this inner act that these successful patients were doing into the practice of Focusing.

Eight years ago, Liz, my former research student, and her husband Cliff, took a gap year at Plum Village in France where they came across the practice of Focusing. Interestingly, instead of bringing me back a book by Thich Nhat Hanh, the founder of Plum Village, Liz gave me Gendlin's little book, *Focusing*. I read it but didn't manage to experience its transformative effects.

A few years later, someone by the name of PC was offering courses in Focusing. I took two courses from him and started my inner journey of self-discovery with this new-found tool. For me, at that point, the exercise was about psychological awareness rather than being explicitly spiritual. It helped me know more about myself, about my self-centeredness, even my hypocrisy. Focusing was a quick way for me to face squarely and frankly my insecure ego.

My first, most enlightening, focusing experience was on Yakushima Island, at the southern tip of Japan. We were a group of ten, staying in a nice tourist cottage by the seaside. Late at night, ten hours before a storm hit the island, the beach was extraordinarily calm. The full moon was like a mirror, pure silver light in a clear sky. Enormous rain clouds covered the horizon as far as the eye could see. A storm must be gathering there, but mysteriously, the ocean here was smooth and quiet. The tide gently caressed the ash-white sand, the soothing sound eased the tension of the imminent storm. Strange moonlight effects had wrought shining silver edges on the clouds. The stars were shining, the view wide open. This was Kyushu Japan's southernmost island, Yakushima. The weather alert said that high winds would paralyze traffic on the island the following day.

It was around 2:00 a.m. and everybody else was asleep. Standing on a ledge overlooking the beach, a feeling of something solemn yet unknown came over me, as if I was conscious in a dream covered by a gossamer veil. I had a gut feeling that here was a good place to put into practice what I had learned about Focusing. I opened my senses and immersed myself in the immediate moment. In front of me was the panoramic view of the glittering sea. There was an eeriness in the air, despite the deceptively tranquil scene. This state of presence, rich in sensations, was a window into my gradual understanding of the unattended self.

The practice of Focusing starts with a step Gendlin called "clearing a space": be aware of whatever feelings and concerns are coming up, greet them one by one, and put each aside, next to you. With a clear space inside, it is easier to get in touch with the *edge* of the unknown.

Gendlin's idea of an edge is the hidden side of the self we are temporarily unable to recognize, deep in the ocean of the unconscious – those past events we cannot remember, and a variety of painful experiences we do not want to face. The edge is the shoreline of the unknown. It is the partly hidden, partly visible boundary of the unconscious.

Exploring the edge, we are felt-sensing the unknown. Gendlin called Focusing a process in which you make contact with a special kind of internal bodily awareness. He called this awareness a felt sense, which is intuitive, sensory, in the realm of the body:

- "A felt sense is usually not just there, it must form. You have to know how to let it form by attending inside your body. When it comes, it is at first unclear, fuzzy. By certain steps it can come into focus and also change. A felt sense is the body's sense of a particular problem or situation."
- "A felt sense is not an emotion. We recognize emotions. We know when we are angry, or sad, or glad. A felt sense is something you do not at first recognize – it is vague and murky. It feels meaningful, but not known. It is body-sense of meaning."

The calmness before the storm was sharpening my senses. My felt sense came strongly. The picturesque moonlit sky was half covered under a still curtain of prescient clouds. Focusing encourages being gentle with these murky felt senses at the edge of my existence, staying close with patience and tolerance, not being judgmental.

I was presented with unfamiliar moods which I did not evade, or rush to understand. The felt sensing of my edge was the starting point of my inner journey. I felt the weariness of performing the role of pleasing all through the years. Underneath the peacefulness of a harmonious life was a storm of inconceivable turbulence. I could smell decay when I groped towards my hidden self in Yakushima.

I won't go into the details of my issues, suffice it to say that my skillfully managed persona was alienating my feelings and needs to such an extent that I was no longer connected with myself. I thought I was a good husband because of my compliance; but in doing so, I suppressed a lot of resentments towards Teresa. I thought I was a liberal father because Constance was free to explore whatever interested her. It is only very recently that Constance told me that she felt the weight of my high expectations on her; me all unaware. Sadly, my stiffness was alienating her. I thought I was a humble scholar, but deep down I was judgmental and jealous.

I considered these sentiments incompatible with my perceived self and forcefully brushed them under the carpet. Out of sight, out of mind. Being a nice guy was fine, but when overdone, I came close to a state of desolation, believing my persona was my good self. It is like wearing a theatrical mask, performing a socially acceptable role, and mistaking the mask for the real me. All my attention was given to maintaining the mask, at the expense of the wellbeing of the flesh and blood behind it.

For the two years after the trip, many of my suppressed feelings began to unfold. It was a prolonged and painstaking process to get out of the dark tunnel of my depression.

The Parachute

I am grateful to have recovered before my daughter's depression worsened into a big crisis. With the experiences of my own recovery, and the practice of Focusing, I was able to reconnect with her and lend her a helping hand. When I put my stiffness aside, she found me much more approachable. At that time, she might have sensed my changes. When her suffering became intolerable, she decided to reach out to me.

I remember one poignant summer night, eight years ago. Teresa was already asleep. I was alone in the living room. Constance came back home in her jogging suit, sweating all over, frazzled. She broke down in tears, saying, "I can't go on like this anymore."

I was shocked, because like me, Constance had been strong, presentable, and independent. Even though she had been depressed for years, Teresa and I had had no clue of her dire condition like sleeping only for two to three hours every night for a few years. She had been putting on her good-girl persona and performing it well. She had held her breath for too long, until she could not hold it any longer. For the first time, Constance told me that she had been suffering from insomnia, high anxiety, an eating disorder, and depression ever since she graduated and started working. She had bruised her knees because of over-exercising and couldn't jog anymore. She had messed up her hormonal cycle because of her strict diet. From that night on, Teresa and I have been accompanying her on a long road of recovery.

Constance started to see a clinical psychologist once a week. For years her eating disorder and depression had been dragging on – three steps forward and two steps back. The good thing is that we, as a family, have rebuilt trust among ourselves. Constance has felt comfortable enough to be willing to share with us her pains and sorrows.

As I discovered more about her suffering, the burden on me became heavier and heavier. I reached a crippling point four years ago, when Constance first told me about her suicidal thoughts. They usually crept into her mind before going to bed. It was so vivid that I felt shivers down my spine listening to her taut voice: images flashing involuntarily in her mind of her jumping from the roof of a tall building, the wind whipping through her fluttering shirt, feeling the pull of gravity and the gust of wind on her face, body plunked to the ground, bone shattered. A graphic sight, no pain, but piercing fear…

Constance's psychologist suggested that she see a psychiatrist and take medication, which she was very reluctant to do at first, until we reached a life-threatening crisis.

I received a call from Constance at noon. This was odd, as she seldom called during the day when she was busy at work. Despite her illness and her youth, she was heading a team of a few dozen staff at that time. There was a whooshing sound of the wind at the end of the phone and my heart filled with lead.

Her voice, trembling, "Dad, can we talk? ... I am on the rooftop..."

A part of me was frozen, chilled all through my spine; another part of me was barely able to stay calm. I thought to myself, how lucky that she called, and that I hadn't missed the call; that I had picked up the phone immediately.

To distract us both, I started talking about trivial things, asking about the work she had done that morning, etc. Then I asked her to leave the railing at the edge and walk back to the staircase.

We stayed on the phone until she was calm and easy.

Hanging up. I collapsed in a heap on the floor, totally exhausted. Teresa was by my side. "We need to stay strong," I whispered.

I rushed to Constance's office and met her alone, holding her hands, telling her I would always be on her side. With her permission, I informed one of her trusted colleagues about her condition and asked the colleague to keep an eye on her. I called Constance's psychologist at once and she referred me to a psychiatrist and an appointment was quickly arranged.

Constance agreed to take medication.

Dr. Wang, the psychiatrist, was a gentle lady in her 40s. She was generous in giving us ample time to talk about Constance's condition. She won Constance's trust by sharing her empathy for suicidal patients, how painful and desperate they are, and how strong the emotional pull is that makes ending one's life seem to be the only thing to do. She told Constance that for her suicidal patients, "There is no alternative in their mind. Death is the only way out." In many ways, Dr. Wang could connect with the feelings deep inside Constance. She told her, "With patience, recovery is possible." Taking medication gradually took effect. Constance's routine of rehearsing suicide before bedtime subsided.

A few months later, Constance told me about a strange dream she'd had of falling from a high place in super slow motion, with stylistic camera angles. She was an onlooker, no fear, no pain. It was like watching an art film by the acclaimed director Wong Kar-wai. The dream alerted me of a possible relapse. "Is Constance on the edge again?" I asked Dr. Wang anxiously. But she gently explained that there was no need for alarm. The dream was qualitatively different from involuntary suicidal thoughts. Those aestheticized images in her dream, coming out of her unconscious, were her defense, drawing a distance between her life and the imagined tragedy.

Going through the challenges in those eventful months, I had learned a great lesson too. All of us face life choices of our own. No matter how much I care about Constance, I can't take her place and bear the suffering for her. Even if she decides to end her life, that's her decision. All I can do is stay by her side and be an empathic companion, providing her with all the support I can give. In the depths of desperation, the pull of self-destruction seems inescapable, but with the company of loved ones, life is a bit bearable and healing is possible.

Some time afterward, Constance had yet another interesting dream: she was falling off the roof, and in mid-air she felt tired, very tired. She asked herself, "Why not pull open the parachute and take a rest?"

In the dream, as soon as she had that idea it became true. A magic bling, a parachute wide open, filled up fully. The sky was blue. White marshmallow clouds were close at her fingertips. She was resting peacefully up in the air.

I remember still, the whole week after she told me that parachute dream, every time I thought of a blue parachute, with a swoosh it would open fully.

Dreamwork

Three years ago, Liz introduced me to a group of friends from all walks of life, who have been meeting regularly ever since. The practice of Focusing brings us all together. The group is led by a teacher called Ed. A devoted Catholic in his early 70s, he is open to Buddhist thoughts and other spiritual practices. Besides teaching Focusing, he has led a few dream workshops, mainly in the Jungian tradition.

When I was in my 30s, I was fascinated by Carl Jung's ideas on dreams. I attended some courses in dream interpretation but found I was getting nowhere. Ed rekindled my interest in dreams. Under his mentorship, I have been recording my dreams in a diary and attending a monthly dream workshop with a group of Focusing friends. Working on dreams has unlocked another door to an enigmatic, expressive, and uninhibited world in which some shadowy sides of me can be unveiled. Dreams embody abundant resources for my individuation, a key term coined by Jung, referring to the process of the life-long journey into the unconscious to attain better understanding of ourselves. Working with Constance on her dreams has also facilitated a few major breakthroughs in her recovery, for dreams help her face squarely the traumas she has been avoiding for years.

In dream literature, there are three main types of dreams: firstly, the "little dreams". They are residues of the waking life, and mostly of little analytic value. They are here for the processing of everyday emotions and experiences.

Secondly, the "blockage dreams", or "compensatory dreams". They are latent imageries of suppressed feelings, traumas, and blockages. They compensate for the one-sidedness of our waking life. If we are facing too much towards the bright side of life, dreams tell us there are shadows at the back of our mind. The unconscious persistently sends signals to the conscious side until the messages manage to get through the bottleneck to facilitate self-awareness and personal growth.

Thirdly, the "big dreams", or archetypal dreams, through which the personal is connected with the collective unconscious. Accumulated throughout human civilization is a big reservoir of mythic images and imageries, which reveal themselves in big dreams to articulate some significant issues about the dreamer as well as society at large.

I have been working on a lot of blockage dreams which help me, and also Constance, to know more about our hidden selves. Of the three types, the most unfathomable is the category of "big dreams". They are often dismissed by academic scholars as mystical fantasies. I remain a skeptic, pondering upon the impossibility of centuries-old images permeating time and space. It is quite remarkable and improbable that a dreamer would dream of these mythic images, which are beyond their personal life.

Added to my curiosity is my research interest in collective memory. Throughout my academic career, I have studied how social and commercial interests produce traditions and histories in their favor, and how people share emotions and myths under the common social conditions of the times. Since the COVID outbreak in 2020, K-Town, the city where our family lives, has undergone colossal changes in which collective emotions are reconstructed and social history rewritten. The impacts of the pandemic were felt on a global scale. Many K-Town citizens share the edginess and stress as the social fabric is torn and rebuilt in the tumult of transition.

Societal and family ties are transforming. According to various surveys, cases of depression and PTSD have been on the rise. It is understood that collective emotions will find their way into dreams, in which the hopes and fears are bigger than those of the individual dreamer. I have experienced this in my own dreams, and occasionally Constance has in hers. I am not sure whether these could be called "big dreams" in the Jungian sense. The dream images I have had are not clearly archetypal, but nevertheless, they are beyond my personal experiences.

The Dream of the Three-headed Dragon

I had a strange dream in which people were left adrift at sea and passing through huge train stations. The most striking image was a scene of the open sea in ultramarine blue. Sharp colors; bright sunlight; exotic landscape. Plaguing the shore was a three-headed dragon, the size of a man, wriggling out of the shell-serrated caves.

When I woke up, my mind was on the alert. I was puzzled by the dragon figure – a mythic creature appearing in my dream for the first time. I flipped through Jung's books on dreams, where he stated that the sea is the symbol of the collective unconscious. We often see the surface, which reflects the sky, but cannot easily see into the depths. Without any empirical support, these kinds of claims can't satisfy the inquiring mind. The dragon symbol by the sea was intriguing.

I was eager to know more about the mythical nature of my dream, so I invited my teacher and friends to work on the dream with me. We met via Zoom and I started with a scene-by-scene description:

I am at the busiest intersection of subway lines on K-Town Island, looking for a train home. In a huge transit hall, hundreds of passengers are walking hurriedly towards their respective platforms. I follow the signs on the wall and on the ground, leading me away from the crowd to an empty site where things start to become surreal. Half-built bridges hang in mid-air, steel rods exposed, loose bits of concrete and cracks everywhere, water dripping down from the soaring ceilings.

I stray through an exit that opens onto the shore. Suddenly I am facing a vast blue sea. The sunlight is so bright that everything is glittering: the deep blue sky, the ultramarine water, choppy white waves, the rocky yellowish shore. Everything is rich in color and real, leaving a crisp impression very different from the usual hazy images of my other dreams. I am thrilled. It's as if I am having a vacation in an exotic tourist destination like those in the Mediterranean Sea.

I board a small boat with a dozen passengers. The boat sails through the water and heads towards a rocky beach, where there is another entrance to the subway. We keep away from the swift currents by staying close to the shore. Still, the wobbling boat is precariously exposed to the waves and gusty wind. A subway trip back home has become a risky boat ride in the open sea. It feels more like an escape.

The boat reaches the shore and stops by the broken stern of a wrecked ship. I get off, bewildered by the primordial landscape. Then a three-headed dragon emerges from between the rocks. The situation is not life-threatening but the creature looks malicious. It is not as huge as those in popular myths, but big enough to inflict a savage mauling from its razor-sharp teeth. As I look closely at the porous caves of the rocky shore, countless other dragons are hidden inside. I can only peep into the darkness, in which parts of the wriggling serpents are vaguely in sight.

I wrench myself out of the risky situation and make my way to the other entrance, which leads me back to a mega-sized train terminal with dozens of parallel tracks and platforms. Trains are pulling in; some rails are empty. I saw a friendly, heavily built station master. I rush towards him, asking, "Which platform is for Santoni (my home district in K-Town)?" "Platform 6," he answers. "How can I get there?"

He leads me to a moving conveyor cutting across the tracks, bridging the opposite platforms. He teaches me to moonwalk on the belt, with my back facing the platform I want. In this strange way, this big guy walks backward to the other side of the track with ease. I try, but the conveyor I'm standing on is moving and pulling me away. I lose my balance. Platform 6 is beyond my reach. I wake up.

This is what we do in our dream workshops: the dreamer narrates his or her dream in the present tense, and includes the feelings that go with it, as I did above. Other members ask questions, point to some unattended parts of the story, and ask the dreamer to elaborate. Often members will share dreams and life stories that are relevant to the dream under scrutiny. This sharing and questioning can usually broaden the dreamer's scheme of interpretation, but the imageries and metaphors of the dream lie within the unconscious of the dreamer, who is the only person capable of uncovering the hidden layers of meanings. Jung argued that intrusive interpretation suggested by "experts" might even lead the believing dreamer away from his or her own unconscious world. Dreams have to be interpreted by the dreamer him/herself.

After listening to my dream, my friends resonated strongly, not with the dragon but with the mood of drifting on the journey. To my surprise, three out of the five friends had had similar dreams recently.

A few days previously, Alfred, a middle-aged engineer, dreamed of himself as an old man who had a child with him, and he couldn't find the platform for the homebound train. He lost all his belongings and was disoriented. Suddenly, a train dashed through the station at high speed, bringing a strong gust of wind that washed over his whole body. He stood there, frozen, in despair.

Bonnie had had a strange dream too. She couldn't catch a train, so she walked to the next station, but still couldn't get on. She then walked into a house, full of her relatives, all busy cleaning up messy stuff scattered everywhere. To her surprise, she was carrying the mattress of her bed all along, walking from one train station to another and up to this messy house.

Samuel recalled yet another similar dream. He was on a small boat in a rough sea. Waves were surging. He was trying, in vain, to catch up with a big ship not far away from his dangerously wavering boat. The big ship was fast, his small boat was slow. He couldn't catch up. Seeing the ship disappearing, he woke up in fear.

Everyone in the group had had some experience of being lost in big transit stations. This was the point where my dream crossed with those of my friends. However, the three-headed dragon didn't evoke a thing in them. They were curious about the reason I was so eager to call up the Zoom meeting.

Ed, our teacher, said he remembered a few years ago, when I first attended his dream workshop, I asked about Jung's concept of the collective unconscious. Stepping back a bit, I was aware of my obsession to validate the mysticism in my dream, which has been a blockage in me for a long time. I am attracted to mystical experiences but my training in analytic thinking, as well as my persona as a researcher, inhibits me from subscribing to things and ideas beyond empirical evidence.

Putting the three-headed dragon aside, there is a conspicuous motif of people adrift on the road and the open sea, which is collective in the sense that it is a shared sentiment for my friends as well as for the people of K-Town at large. Many have left the city. We all have loved ones, relatives and friends who have migrated to other countries within a very short period. We are adrift, for real and in our mind.

Bonnie's dream is pregnant with symbolic meaning. The mattress, so intimate a belonging in her domestic space, was being carried on the road. In Alfred's dream he lost his belongings and was left behind on the platform. And Samuel was exposed to danger in the stormy sea. The shared sentiments in the dreams might not be as "archetypal" as Jung had emphasized.

Nevertheless, a wide range of sentiments are shared collectively at this historical juncture

The motif of being adrift on the journey in my dream is self-explanatory, except for two odd bits – the dragon and the backward movement of the station master. We, as a group, wanted to put the dragon aside. (It was only after a year that the dragon revealed its colors).

My friends were curious about the ending of the dream, with me wanting to go to platform 6 for home, but not being able to because the moonwalk on the conveyer was too difficult for me. They asked me to pay attention to the details of the scene in the train station. So, I tried.

I started by describing the attire and demeanor of the station master: uniform of blue, with a white cap, tall, heavily built, gentle, and agile. As I focused on his way of presenting his moonwalk steps, the most intriguing thing was that he demonstrated his awkward and illogical way of walking as if it was normal, easy, straightforward, and commonsensical.

All characters and images originate from the dreamer. In Jungian analysis, the dream ego (the me in the dream) is the dreamer. The villain and the supporting characters are also constructed by the dreamer. One of the tools of dreamwork is to step into the shoes of these side characters and look into the dream world from their perspective. If I were the station master, I would be doing something I wouldn't do in my waking life. The normal me would be very uncomfortable behaving awkwardly, like walking backward; being nonsensical would be too embarrassing. The dream ego, just as the waking me, was acting normally. It seems that the unacceptable side of me, in the disguise of the station master, was quite agile in my dream. If I were to see the dream through his eyes, moving forward or backward wouldn't be a problem at all. It's as easy as doing some dance steps.

It reminded me of a great lesson in the practice of Focusing, that pausing is in fact a step on the way forward. Pausing for a while, looking into oneself, reflecting on the age-old habit of doing things in a familiar pattern. The pause allows a great opening for change.

Sharon suggested that I walked like the station master, re-visiting the dream in reverse. Instead of single-mindedly wanting to go home, I could pay more attention to the situation immediately around me.

So, I followed her suggestion and found that my sense of loss was significantly lessened. I acted like the station master, feeling at home at the station. Going backward onto the boat, the fellow passengers I'd previously not noticed came into focus. I shared a feeling of brotherhood with the people on the same boat.

Back at the ruins of the transit station at the beginning of the dream, I felt the solemnness of the crossroads I was at, the historic juncture, unforgettable, us all adrift with a nostalgia for the bygone years of our life, longing to go home.

A Follow-up

After the Zoom meeting, I had another dream a few days later. Teresa, Constance and I were on the road with a few dozen people. A disabled guy was running clumsily with a crutch. We were all in a hurry. It was tense.

Taking shelter in a big building, I bumped into a colleague in a hideout under a flight of stairs. In real life he always wears a suit and tie – he is a tech geek from a well-off family. He was now, in my dream, a homeless person by choice. He stayed in this hideout far away from his luxurious home. I've been overly prudish all my life and feel uncomfortable sharing intimate feelings with others, but in the dream I did something unusual for me. I hugged him. He was thrilled to see me in this awkward place.

In my dream, I knew the difficulties he had been through. I wished him well and bid him farewell. "Stay," he said, with tears in his eyes, "I have a lot of things I want to share with you." I stayed, tears rolling down my face.

Without the pause and re-orientation of my perspective in the previous Zoom meeting, I probably wouldn't have had this follow-up dream. Even if I did dream about this professional-turned-homeless colleague, I wouldn't have shared that intimate moment with him. Many of the sufferings we face won't have a readily available solution, but being an empathetic companion is always a precious gift that we can share with each other.

Many of us are in the process of making sense of the big change we have been experiencing. My dreams, as well as the dreams of Bonnie, Alfred, and Samuel, are a microcosm of a collective sentiment of leaving home and finding our way back.

Thinking and Writing at the Edge

In the summer of 2020, I took a course on *Thinking at the Edge* from Lou, Ed's teacher. At first, I thought this Thinking at the Edge (TAE) course was another version of Focusing. I soon learned that TAE is a combination of felt sensing and analytic thinking. I had watched a few video clips on TAE previously but hadn't registered its relevance. I do know about Gendlin's philosophy of knowing by felt-sensing the emerging ideas from the implicit. According to him, this is where new and unique knowledge can originate. That said, I had no idea how TAE could be applied to my life. Amusingly, I was caught by a strong sense of synchronicity in the first Zoom session.

For a few months before meeting Lou, I had been experimenting with a new mode of writing. Whereas before, when writing my column I would plan ahead, sometimes point by point, and have a preconceived structure, I had started to wait for something to unfold before me. This involved some elements of Focusing, waiting for something written upon my senses, and writing from that something I feel at the moment. The writing process is not clear to me yet. The only word to describe it is WAIT.

Right at the very beginning of the course, when Lou explained the basics of TAE, it dawned on me that "Thinking at the Edge" was exactly what I needed at that juncture – to write not in the analytic mode but to write from a felt sense. At the time I didn't know that this new way of writing I acquired from TAE would be applied to writing this book. Throughout the six Zoom sessions I focused on the words "anticipatory waiting", exploring the rich meanings behind my weekly writing ritual by checking back and forth with concepts and felt senses.

In Lou's classes, we paid attention to the small details in our daily routines. Most of us had been practicing Focusing for a long while. As for me, a beginner, I was interested in relating focusing to my previous experiences in research and teaching. Before my retirement, I taught qualitative research methodology for many years and did quite a lot of ethnographic studies. I noticed that focusers and ethnographers are both trained to attune to the minute sensations, stimuli and feelings of the situation, with focusers being more aware of the way in which bodily sensations lead us from the known to the edge of the unknown.

Sometimes I borrowed Heidegger's concept of Being-in-the-world (Dasein) when I discussed with my research students the assumptions of ethnography. In any given situation, the ethnographer is not an isolated and objective observer, s/he is embedded in the field, interacting with the things and people s/he is researching. The inter-penetrative nature of Being-in-the-world is the foundation of ethnographic understanding. There is a little bit of you in me; there are some bits of the world in me too. Being-in-the-world is extensively vast, and it is also privatively minute, inside the implicit realm of the individual body.

In a way, ethnography is compatible with Focusing and TAE. It takes seriously the contradictions and complexities of human existence. Ethnographers present their findings in what they call a "thick description", an approach originated by British philosopher Gilbert Ryle in 1968 and theorized by American anthropologist Clifford Geertz in his 1973 article, "Thick Description: Toward an Interpretive Theory of Culture". It is a writing style which attends to physical details as well as the inner process of meaning-making. It acknowledges firstly that some ambiguities in social interactions are unresolvable, and secondly that social understanding is achievable without a compact theoretical closure.

Dasein, or Being-in-the world, is the philosophical base for thick ethnographic description. For Focusing, it is an embodied practice. Felt senses emerge from within the somatic, while bodies are situated in life worlds. We bear the imprints of our time and each individual marks his or her life story onto the world. Thus, Focusing is the rudimentary, the very basic step of knowing the somatic coding of the experiential world. TAE, as a way of *thinking at the edge,* seeks to find new vocabularies for untold experiences. Thick description, as a way of *writing at the edge,* is an operational tool for TAE to bring the implicit to the explicit realm of comprehension, without diluting the implicitness of human experiences.

Lou worked with us on the first five steps of TAE. The first step of TAE is to "choose something you know and cannot yet say, that wants to be said". Each of the eight of us had different ideas to work on: doing voluntary work, engaging in therapy and counseling, trying out a new working style, being more active in building up friendships, etc. Then we spelled out the public meanings of the keywords in our project. It was a fruitful exercise when we checked these public meanings with our felt senses and recognized "that's not what I meant". Then, we tried to describe these meanings in full, using fresh language unique to us individually.

Lou concluded our class by sharing Gendlin's idea of the divine call. The felt sense of an individual can be seen as part of this call. It is a unique invitation and can't be fleshed out by any other human being on earth. Thinking at our own unique edges of the moment, it is raw, new, and exceeds all existing vocabularies. If articulated, it is a gift to us and the world. However small, it is a contribution to humanity.

Chapter 2

The Funeral of the Sacrificial Lamb

The Cow Is Strong

Some weeks ago, I dreamed of a hasty taxi trip to a trans-border train station. We rode past a ranch, which was in terrible condition – the cows were covered in mud, dirt and their own excrement. The taxi took me to a train platform. Under my arm I carried the body of a dead lamb, shaved clean. I was supposed to take the train somewhere to attend a peace offering ritual.

This dream stuck in my mind, without a clue of what it meant. It was not until a few months later that the dream played out in my waking life, like a fable slowly unveiling. From the depths of my unconscious a flower blooms, showing its thirty stamens in silence. In ruins and rubble, softly sung hymns could be heard from afar.

The dream contained big contrasts – the ranch was messy, but the station platform was clean and neat. The cows were struggling, while a dead lamb rested in peace. The cows were confined, but I was leaving of my own free will. I was not caught in the inhumane mess of the ranch.

Repulsive scenes in dreams more often than not represent latent concerns that the conscious mind is unaware of. Strong symbols are conspicuous, as if they are yelling at the dreamer, demanding attention. The most disgusting scene in this dream was a cow shitting directly onto the taxi window. A rancher invited me to get out of the taxi and take a look at the beautiful scenery. But in the dream, the ranch was a messy cattle farm. I ignored the rancher.

Something strange was troubling me. I had an eerie feeling inside. The ranch, repulsive to me, might be something I had repressed. Is the ranch a destination that I should visit? Should

I pay more attention to the cows instead of just passing by? Isn't it my wish to share the burdens of those who are suffering? As days went by, I had a prescient feeling about the dream. The inhumane confinement of the cattle was something I had avoided facing. I hid inside a taxi. Was the dream a premonition for me personally? Was I the cow? Or was it my unconscious wish to stay away from pain and suffering?

I plucked up the courage to work on the dream by having a session of Focusing with Cliff. I closed my eyes and sank deep into the dream. I described my bodily sensations. Cliff repeated my descriptions and reported to me what he observed about my facial expressions, posture, etc. The cow, with its messy hide, came to my mind. I got closer and petted its forehead. I said, "What a pity..." Cliff repeated, "What a pity! That's what you said to the cow." To my surprise, when I touched its head, a completely opposite feeling surged up, a strong sensation, full of life and energy. "What a pity" was a complete mismatch. The cow in the dream, despite all odds, was thriving. I was moved by its determination to flourish. It was the sensation of a shift, like a car shifting gear.

Shifting is not an unusual feeling in Focusing. When our conscious mind looks only at one side of the coin, a sudden awareness of the coin having another side will trigger a bodily sensation that focusers call a shift. Eating and shitting, the basics of living. Mud and lotus, two sides of a coin. Re-experiencing the dream, I realized the opposite side of my repulsive reaction to the cows. I was underestimating resilience and avoiding suffering. Condescendingly, I was looking at the trapped creatures with pity and sadness. Those from the outside feel sorry for those trapped inside their miseries and misfortunes. For the insiders, some fall, some survive, some become stronger, and quite a few of them turn sufferings into blessings. I have known of survivors who are resilient like a cactus, compassionate like a lotus, much stronger than the onlookers who haven't experienced things first-hand.

The reversal of the dream went much further. The cows, in their messiness, became a symbol of endurance. The sacrificial lamb, with all its peacefulness, became a symbol of fear for me.

A month after I had the dream, some insiders warned me that the investment company that housed the CSR initiative had been entangled in a big financial dispute. Colossal debts had been incurred. I had no knowledge of the details, but the risk seemed to loom large. The dream symbol of the lamb quickly revealed its color. As an offering, the lamb had to sacrifice itself, shed its blood, to pay the toll vicariously for the community. According to my rational mind, seeing myself as that sacrificial lamb was a nonsensical idea and without any empirical ground. But that was exactly my fear, suppressed so deep at the back of my mind that I dared not bring it up for examination. The lamb, resting peacefully in my dream, became a symbol of my worst fear.

Cape O, the Refuge

Turmoil intensified. Someone arranged a meeting for myself and Brian with a former consultant of the initiative. We talked about trivial matters for a while, like friends catching up with this and that of our whereabouts and recent engagements. Then out of nowhere, this distant friend whispered, "You guys better liquidate the subsidiary company as soon as possible." I sensed the seriousness of this and immediately agreed.

I was informed that all the previous consultants had resigned. As newcomers, Brian and I didn't know much about the finance of the CSR initiative before we arrived, not to mention the huge investment operations of the parent company. We were the only two remaining in the CSR subsidiary, like naked antennas exposed in open air, we could be struck by lightning anytime in the storm. We asked for an immediate close down. I anxiously waited for the end of the grace period so that the company could be liquidated and cleared of any possible risk associated with the parent company. It was an anxious wait.

To ease my anxiety, I went for a hike by myself, along the trail from Eastern Creek to Cape O, the fishing village at the far west corner of K-Town. In the 1970s, in my teens and before the satellite town was built, this serene seaside trail had been my favorite hideout. I went there countless times, when I felt lost, when I had a big life decision to make. Sunsets in Cape O were so memorable with Teresa, sitting at the breakwater watching the big red sun sinking into the sea. This was some 40 years ago. Eastern Creek was a sleepy hamlet then, with only a few hundred inhabitants. Now it is a lively satellite town with a population of more than a hundred thousand. However, off I hiked for just half an hour into the ancient trail. I found tranquility, away from the city, lush green all along, with cool shade under the trees.

I walked past some deserted villages of brick huts and small cottages. Most of them were in ruins with only the walls maintaining the shape of houses – roofs collapsed, windows broken, weeds and vines filling up the ruin inside. But it was comforting to see that a few villagers had come back, or had never left their well-managed cabins and lodges. Some even had beds of flowers and vegetable fields in their backyards.

I was in a state of agitation. These lodges became desirable objects to me. I thought to myself that if I could lead a life of seclusion in a hidden refuge like the one in front of me, away from the boiling city, the chaos caused by the pandemic and all the risks out there, I would be blessed. Of course, this fantasy burst like a soap bubble when I thought twice. Unless I could live without a phone or computer, I would be found even if I were living in a cave without an address. There is no escape in contemporary society with electronic monitoring so precise and extensive.

Anxiety is like a tidal wave. The harder I wanted to block my trepidation, the stronger it grew. Walking alone was good. My emotions were easily released to the surface. Yet, when facing unexpected difficulties, what came to the surface was the question "what if?" What if I had rejected the invitation right away with a reasonable excuse? Then I wouldn't have been forced to endure such suffocating anxiety.

Over the years, I have learned to be gentler with myself and to let grievances come through and leave them there. Walking along the trail, a part of me was stuck in regret, but there was another part of me filled with compassion and conviction. This is what Gendlin called "clearing a space" – a space for me to recall my original intent: that I am here to help, to provide support for those in distress, to make peace, to heal. This has been my aspiration and mission all through my life.

When I was a teenager, I used to come here alone in the late evening, taking the last ferry, arriving at the pier of Cape O at midnight. I usually wandered along the empty alleys for a while whilst the whole fishing village was asleep. It was somewhat like entering a twilight zone, experiencing an otherworldly calmness very different from the hustle of the city.

When the sailors left, I went back to the pier and spent the night inside the empty ferry. It was quiet. The stars were bright and silvery. I remembered I had once made a wish that I would be of some worth to this world and felt that all the shiny stars were paying extra attention to my vow.

Fond memories calmed me down. When there was a bigger space inside of me, fear and anxiety became moderate. A small group of close friends who knew of my situation had been very supportive. "Just want to say we are here with you, and you are a good person. And you are not alone, and we all care about you," was a heartwarming message that one of them had sent me.

It had rained a few days ago. The water running through the brook was high. There were small whirlpools in between boulders, babbling and glittering under the midday sun. This serenity was otherworldly. I was moved. In just a brief period, my secure life had been shattered. It seemed that there was a hole in my soul. Circumstances are swiftly changing and we can't hold on to the things we love and hold dear at heart, just like the brook can't hold on to the running water. Yet the water is intimately in touch with everything it flows through – it won't stay, but the brook is here throughout the ages. At that moment, the running water spoke softly of its beauty and gentleness, which reverberated deep inside of me. This was the same scenic trail I had visited 40 years ago. I had a nostalgic sadness, a sense of loss, but at the same time a gratifying tranquility, given generously to me, then and now.

My Cat Goes Blind

My worst fear was realized on 4th November 2021. Two private investigators arrived with a legal document. No more speculation. This was before we had had a chance to liquidate the subsidiary company, our case was wide open and out of our hands.

As the investigators stood at the doorstep, my cat Mui was acting strangely. She hated strangers. Every time the doorbell rang, she would dash for her hide-out. This time, despite the pungent cologne the investigators were wearing, she lay on the dining table in front of the door, staring at them. And she stayed there like a frozen statue until they left.

That evening Mui started to stumble when she walked, as if she couldn't see. For the past few years she has slept most of the time during the day, as old cats do. But in the days after the visit she was tense and stayed awake all the time.

A couple of weeks earlier our family, already nerve-wracked, knowing that I was under investigation, noticed that Mui had a swelling on her lower eyelid. We took her to the vet where some anomalies in her stomach were discovered and cancer was suspected. A check-up was scheduled later in the week. She had been in robust health, seldom needing to see a vet, but within a week her condition had turned critical.

I worried about her. I had a hunch that she would die. Meanwhile, I was busy meeting lawyers handling our case. The suspected financial fraud was complicated – there were two camps involved. The ones from the parent company were in the spotlight, with Brian and me in a supporting role. Brian is a scholar in Chinese Classics. Like me, he is participating in a voluntary capacity; a social service, as we see it.

On the day of the investigators' visit, I went hiking in the morning, and joined the meeting with the lawyers in the late afternoon.

On my way to the Central Business District of the city, my anxiety caught me tight at the throat and chest. What was most unsettling was the apprehension of a bottomless pit that Brian and I were falling into. We were quite ignorant of what the parent company had been doing. We had accepted the invitation out of goodwill to serve the community.

Taking the subway, I was so exhausted by the nerve-wracking uncertainty that I had to sit down for a rest on a bench on the platform. Trains were dashing in, the rush of the cool gust whirling in the air. I was able to ground myself on the sights around me, a wide display of sound, sight and sensations. A young mother was carefully pushing a baby stroller through the crowd. A Filipino maid was talking on her phone. Some school kids were chatting cheerfully while getting off the train. Most numerous were well dressed businessmen and women walking past in great haste, totally absorbed in whatever busy business they were in.

The familiar voice of the subway Tannoy echoed with the sound of the incoming and departing trains. "Please stand back from the doors." "Please mind the gap between the train and the platform." This voice has been with most K-Town citizens for decades, hearing the same female voice whenever we travel on the subway. A strange nostalgia was gently replenishing my anxiety-ridden heart. The city had given me so much – my career, my friends, the city's cultural diversity...

At the meeting, the lawyer representing the parent company said he had been my student many years ago in a General Education course with an enrollment of a hundred students. Of course I couldn't remember him as my former student, it was almost two decades ago; however he had shown me a human touch, which eased my heart. He pointed out that Brian and I were not on the radar. The main targets were the core members of the parent investment company. According to him even the core members were not aware of the financial loopholes that led them into the dispute. Since legally there was a conflict of interest between the two of us and the others, we were advised to leave the meeting and find another representing lawyer. No more contact between the two groups. From now on Brian and I were on our own.

A Mountain Upside Down

We met with our own lawyers, who painted a very different picture. My former student, the lawyer of the parent company, had said the day before that we were not on the radar, but our lawyers pointed out that the case was so complicated and obscure that they couldn't say anything about what might happen to us. The financial corporation pressing charges is aggressive, the more extensive they make the case, the larger amount of money they could reclaim.

We were given a very tight schedule of only 12 days to go through tons of documents. I didn't have time to attend to my emotional upheaval, there were so many things going on at the same time. Leaving the lawyers' office, Brian and I were both anxious. Brian is a devoted Buddhist. He went to his friend, Candice, who is well versed in I Ching, *the Book of Change,* an ancient Chinese classic on divination. Candice made two divinations for him. The oracle for Brian was to lay low, like a mountain buried upside down, taking refuge underground. Another divination about how the initiative would implicate him was graphic and specific: "A fire breaks out of the secret depths of the earth, blazing up to the toes. They must immediately leave the carriage, forget belongings, and walk away." The advice was to leave and walk out of the situation.

The divination was for Brian, not for me, but since our situation was the same Brian advised me to cut off all my social engagements. It was wise advice. So, in just half an hour I cancelled my newspaper columns all at once.

It was 7:00 pm in the evening. I parked my car at the same spot where I received the call inviting me to join the initiative eight months ago, and waited for my daughter to get off from work. While waiting, I sent several messages to the editors and organizers to inform them of my decision. I was surprised by my own determination. The most difficult termination was of the column I had written for more than two decades. But in view of the danger I was in, I sent the editor a farewell note right away.

The Unintended Prayer

Things were happening at such a disorienting speed that I didn't have the luxury of contemplating the connections between the hectic events. But one thing was overshadowing all others – the dream of the sacrificial lamb. Was I the scapegoat? Was I to be accused and sacrificed? Was the dream a premonition?

In the morning, I visited Cliff for another session of Focusing. Focusing doesn't require the revealing of sensitive details. With mutual trust, the focuser (me) and the companion (Cliff) just need to be fully present and mindful of what emerges from the inside. I calmed myself down in front of Cliff and just let my dream symbols bring out the sensations of the moment we were in.

The dream ego (me-the-dreamer in the dream) and all other objects and characters (including the villain and the monster) are a split self of the dreamer. Whether it be my shadows or sub-personalities, they are all a part of me. But there are exceptions. From the Jungian perspective, mythic symbols can enter dreams from the collective unconscious outside of the dreamer's life. The lamb which had to shed its blood seemed to embody the fear deep inside me. Or, it might be something spiritual that was beyond me. I really didn't know if it was a part of me or if it was from the beyond.

In my meditative state, I took on the role of the lamb, loosened up my body as if I were dead, with my head and arms leaning on the chair, like the neatly slain animal. Cliff's role was essential. He said, "A lamb is resting on the chair." His retelling was like a mirror, helping me to alter my spatial perception.

I felt as if I was sitting amid a chaotic city at the height of a primordial ceremony. I poured my heart out, opened both arms and prayed for the first time in decades. In trembling words, I murmured:

"We are walking through the shadow of death, like a lamb, weak and feeble. We don't know when our nightmares will end. Our despair is as deep as a bottomless pit. We entrust ourselves to you. Our only hope is your deliverance. I lay before you, resting upon your providence. Please remember those in suffering, those who have lost their loved ones. Please remember those carrying the burdens of our time. For those without hope, grant them hope; for those without faith, grant them the courage to believe in your grace; for those without the will to endure, grant them the strength to carry on; for those in bitter acrimonies, grant them reconciliation of the heart. Hear our prayer, please heal our wounds, please bring peace to us all."

Both Cliff and I were surprised by the emotionally loaded outpouring. In fact I found it silly to pray, for if God is benevolent there is no need for us to beg. I hadn't prayed since I left the church decades ago. But at that moment the prayer came out of me with sincerity and a sense of urgency. It was a prayer I didn't fully comprehend. As for Cliff, a Buddhist, the intensity of the prayer puzzled him too. When we were done with the Focusing session he spoke to me, as if he was talking to himself: "This prayer is poignant."

The World Health Organization estimates that 6.9 million deaths have been recorded worldwide since December 2019, but the actual number is thought to be higher. The sacrificial lamb, feeble like feathers, transient like mayflies, offered no significant relief to the suffering of our time. However, I have learned something from this dream through meditative Focusing. It has been a transformation process from apprehension to endurance and compassion. The peace offering is accomplished not by the taking away of suffering and danger, but by kindness and reconciliation.

After the meeting with Cliff I needed to take Mui to the Vet. On the way to the clinic I received a call from my lawyer saying that a team of lawyers, unknown to me, would like to offer their help. A council was arranged on Sunday. I was bewildered by this ad hoc meeting. Why would lawyers volunteer to help?

Constance and I made it to the clinic with Mui at 4:00 pm, where she was given a series of tests. A needle had to pierce her skin in order to take her blood pressure. She hissed fiercely, which was very uncharacteristic of her. I guessed mostly because of her prolonged sleeplessness. The vet told us that Mui's blood pressure had shot up to 200, her retina had fallen off – she couldn't see. Probably her tense condition was the reason why she had been unable to sleep. Given her age, there was a high probability that she had already had a minor stroke, and with her suspected cancer, intrusive testing and an operation were not advisable. After a brief discussion with the vet we decided to put her to sleep. Constance and I were both in tears but we thought this was best for her.

Teresa was in a meeting, and we asked her to hurry up and come to say goodbye to Mui. She arrived at 5:00 pm, tears on her face. The vet injected Mui with a light dose of tranquilizer to ease her tension. Within a few seconds Mui fell asleep. Filling the small room was the sound of her sweet and peaceful snoring. This eased our hearts. After three days of insomnia and great pain she finally got her rest. It was sad to say goodbye but really comforting to see her in such a relaxing deep sleep. At 5:30 the vet injected a high dose of tranquilizer, and we were beside her when her heart ceased to beat.

A guy came to pick her up and take her to the funeral home at 6:00 pm. We drove home. Near the seaside we saw the purplish sky, a magnificent sunset, sunbeams radiating from the far end of the skyline. I parked the car and we went directly to the boardwalk by the sea. In front of this magical and tranquil scene we wished Mui peace and thanked her for sharing with us 16 lovely years together. Constance took a photo and the curtain of night fell quickly, as if Mui was taking a bow, her wonderful life on earth accomplished. This rare and majestic sunset was captured in different parts of the city. Photos were instantly shared on social media, and we felt blessed to have witnessed the moment before it was gone.

A lot of happenings had been compressed in a short period of time – fatigue, stress, sadness, and the feeling of being vulnerable and helpless filled my days. All things taken for granted seemed feeble and transient. Life is short.

An Unexpected Intervention

A well-known barrister, friend of an acquaintance of Brian, intervened. He arranged a council with three other lawyers (including our own) to provide legal advice pro bono. We gathered at his office in the late evening, eight of us altogether. Phones were all collected and sealed in a box. We kept an online news broadcast on, buzzing away in the background to interfere with eavesdropping. The barrister was smart. He came up with the idea of the two of us officially resigning from the company. I wasn't aware of this option and its feasibility, because we were the only two remaining directors. To whom could we submit our resignation? I asked. One lawyer specialized in this area. She said we could do that by submitting a signed letter to the registry.

After a few rounds of keen discussion, we concluded that we would send out a signal of excision from the parent company by immediately stopping signing papers and all other duties. Our resignation would be effective on the same day as we processed all the documents as required. I was a bit relieved with this resolution being worked out, but the barrister still painted an extremely stark picture of the prospects of our case. Our resignation might only lessen our liability.

Brian and I left the meeting with lead-filled hearts. It felt like walking into a nightmarish situation, calm and quiet on the surface, but everything was uncertain and potentially detrimental. That was a Sunday. When the meeting finished it was almost 10:00 pm. The spacious lobby of the building was a hollow vacuum. Outside, the streets were empty. The Central Business District, under the pale bluish lighting was like a deserted movie set on a gigantic scale.

My Mind Goes Blank

The first two weeks of November had been hectic and eventful: My cat died; I attended 4 meetings with different lawyers; I had to assist in the processing of the paperwork as required; and because of stress, I couldn't sleep at night and woke up early. I guessed the alarm system in my biological clock, which was set in the early morning of November 4, had switched on every morning at the same time since then. I was exhausted.

At midnight on November 16, when everything required of me had been done, I received a telephone call from Neil, the long-time secretary handling the company. He had done most of the photocopying and I had been in frequent contact with him over the past week. He uttered from the other end of the phone, "Please don't be scared, I have already left the city. I'm just calling to say goodbye in person. I have been involved much deeper than you. I have to leave. Take care." I guessed the telephone call was made before the plane took off.

The phone conversation with Neil was brief but heavy.

I didn't sleep well and woke up at 5:30 am. All the heavy-duty work was done. Suddenly I had plenty of time to think, but my mind was blank. Tense emotions took charge. I was restless and my attention span was brief. I couldn't concentrate on anything. I had difficulty eating my breakfast. My throat was stiff, and I couldn't swallow a small bite of sandwich. Sensing these symptoms of stress, I decided to take a walk at the country park.

After a half hour's drive I parked my car and started to walk along the seaside. It took me an hour to arrive at Sam's Bay and I was still out of focus and restless. This had never happened to me. The sea, the trees, the majestic mountains always calm me down. An hour of mindful walking should surely bring my racing heart to restful peace. But when I sat beside the pond with a vast meadowland in front of me, I was still in a jittery state, numb to the blue sky and green ridges far in the distance.

Mandy, another lawyer unknown to me, had offered to see me in the evening. Venus, my former research student, had lined up the meeting. I didn't want to meet her in such a state of mind but I was not in control of myself. I tried to meditate, do some Focusing or grounding, but in vain.

The sun was scorching at noon. I couldn't sit still. I needed a shaded area that I could ramble through to ease my stress. It was pleasing to have found big shade under a row of banyan trees, as if as a refuge to shelter me from the unceasing agitation. I walked back and forth under the shade for a while, totally consumed by my chattering mind until I heard a bird squeal, sharp and loud, like a spear thrown through the air. Suddenly, I was awakened to the symphony of birds chirping, twittering, whispering, and singing, which had always been there, only I was too into myself that I had filtered out all the rich texture of the soundscape all around me.

This happened all in split seconds. I found myself in a deep meditative trance. There was no time, only a vast space. All the lovely, precious and memorable moments I spent with my two cats I re-experienced on the spot. It was a strange sensation. I knew both of my cats, Charcoal and Mui, were dead but to me they felt alive, their lifetimes flourished in the here and now. My anxiety melted into thin air. There were tears in my eyes. I felt loved and blessed. I was being taken care of.

The scene of Charcoal dying faded in. He was so weak that he slept on the floor like a piece of soft cotton. I slept on the floor next to him, giving him all my love and gratitude. Mui slept like a log before she passed away. I felt good about her peaceful death, and much gratitude for her loving companionship over the past 16 years. The two cats, the significant moments of their lives, emerged again in my mind – Charcoal's innocent look when he was still a kitten. His purring when he sat on my lap. Mui's big eyes and funny face. Her eccentric way of greeting us when we came back home. I took those warm feelings deep in my heart. They were, and still are, with me all along.

I calmed down. Back to myself, I could think straight.

I got back my ability to enjoy the picturesque meadowland, the tiny cross-shaped white flowers blossoming at every corner of the green, the amazing blue sky, the cheerful white clouds in funny sizes and shapes. I felt peaceful and connected. Throughout my life I have experienced such a shift of consciousness only a few times. Time seemed to have stopped – or there was no sense of time. I guess, the emotional tumult of that week shook up my psyche, hacking out a space to allow this spiritual shift to happen.

I went back home to refresh myself and attend the meeting that Venus had arranged for Brian and me. We met up with Mandy in a private café on the second floor of an old building. In her early 30s, Mandy was casually dressed and was very friendly to us. She knew who we were. This was not surprising since people know who's who in the media and cultural scenes, but what was a surprise was that Mandy knew our situation inside out.

We had submitted our resignations a day ago. She knew about this latest move, and of course she knew the lawyers handling our case and all the people involved. We told her that we had been really stressed out when the barrister told us that in his professional judgement we were surely on the hit list. With an easy smile, she gave us her estimation: our risk was low.

What a relief! The stark projection from the barrister had given us a big push to stop everything immediately, but at the same time left a huge burden on our shoulders. Mandy's estimation eased that burden a lot. Otherwise, the slowly unfolding legal procedure would be a long and tortuous wait. We had two completely opposite projections on our prospects, both offered by experienced and respectable lawyers in the field. This discrepancy rendered our days a bit more bearable but no less stressful.

Jung's Synchronicity

In the 1920s, Carl Jung started to talk about the phenomenon of synchronicity, referring to the connection between psychological and physical reality – for instance, dreaming of a long-forgotten friend and receiving the news of his death the subsequent morning. Two things overlap each other, purely coincidental, but are meaningful to the individual involved.

Jung's most widely quoted example is the story of the scarab beetle. A well-educated lady had been treated by Jung for a long time without any breakthrough. Her rigid and rational mind-set was seen as the bottleneck of the therapeutic process. In a counseling session she said she had dreamed of a scarab-shaped jewel. At that moment a tapping sound came at the window behind Jung. He opened the window and found a beetle, grabbed it in his hand and opened his palm to show it to the client, asking, "Is this beetle the one in your dream?" She was shocked and lowered her defenses, which became the turning point of the therapy.

Jung adopted rigorous analytic language in his academic writings. He was careful not to position himself as an enthusiast of the spiritual realms. His idea of synchronicity, formulated in the 1920s, was finally published in 1952 entitled, *Synchronicity: A Non-Causal Connecting Principle*. Publishing any earlier might not have been compatible with his wish to maintain his identity as a social scientist. He waited until later in his career, when he felt more able to share his understanding of the mythical aspects of life and the world. Synchronicity is one of his original concepts beyond the rational mind. Coincidences are common experiences in our everyday life, related events which are not tied by a causal relation. He asked, aren't there psycho-physical configurations not yet unraveled by men?

Jung's idea of synchronicity has been under critical scrutiny with the rise of its popularity since the 1950s. The famous scarab beetle story, for example, has been criticized for being too hasty as a proof of synchronicity. Firstly, in Zurich where Jung's office was, beetles were common insects. A beetle tapping the window was not that extraordinary an incident. Secondly, it is not uncommon for a client to adopt the words and imageries used by the therapist. Mythical contents might have been suggested by Jung. Thirdly, Jung had the intention of breaking through his client's rational defense mechanism, therefore he was an active participant of the meaning-making process which was not completely random and coincidental. When he cupped the beetle in his palm and handed it to the lady he had an obvious intention of surprising her.

I read both sides of the argument: that synchronicity is statistical occurrence, or that it is meaningful articulation. Taking the position of an agnostic at first, I saw this as one of those phenomena which is outside my experiential capacity to judge whether it exists or not.

However, after what has been happening, synchronicity to me is not a concept anymore. It is a concrete package of grave personal significance. I feel as if there was, and still is, an unseen web threading the imagery in my mind and the events unfolding in the real world. This realization had gradually come to the surface – oddly enough at the funeral of my cat.

The funeral was scheduled for November 24. The staff told us to bring some flowers for the ceremony. Constance, always intuitive, asked us to buy flowers with small petals and in light pink. She just knew that type of flowers matched Mui. Constance had to work, so Teresa and I brought a bunch of carnations to the funeral home, which was situated in a remote factory complex. The venue was peaceful and quiet. We were admitted to a small memorial hall to spend some private time with Mui. She was resting peacefully inside a small basket lined in purple silk. The lady member of staff said Mui had been cleaned up and she was soft – we could pet her as we wished. The memories of Mui filled our minds. Her simple and trusting temperament warmed our hearts.

When I petted her forehead, I realized at once that she was the look-alike of the sacrificial lamb in my dream. Mui had round cheeks as British short-haired cats do, but in her dehydrated state her face became diamond-shaped, with a pointed chin and a pair of closed eyes tilted upward on both sides. It was the face of the lamb in my dream. Her body was as slim as a baby lamb too.

I don't think this is my wanting, nor my make-believe. It wasn't. It was a sudden awareness of the close resemblance that I would never have thought of. The body of the lamb that I held in my dream six months ago was the body of my cat in front of me – its softness, its featherweight, the size and shape of her face, all felt the same. With this sudden handle of the felt sense, many dots linked together to become an intriguing web.

- The dream triggered some undefined anxiety. The symbols of the cow and the sacrificial lamb gave a vague impression of the situation I was facing.
- My cat went blind the day the investigators visited. She died three days later. She had been very healthy until then.
- In a Focusing session right before her death, I immersed myself in the symbol of the lamb. Responding to an erratic urge, I made a sincere prayer for those in grave suffering. I hadn't prayed for more than 20 years, yet words came through naturally.
- Immediately after the Focusing session, on the way home to take my cat to the vet, I received a phone call informing me that a barrister would like to help. Promptly arranged was a meeting that changed the course of events: we decided to resign and stop everything immediately.
- Right after Mui passed away, while driving home, there was a magnificent sunset we had rarely seen. I stopped the car and we got to the waterfront and paid tribute to Mui before the setting sun. Constance took a picture of the sky in crimson red and purplish blue.

- As a token of thanks, I sent the picture to my editor to say goodbye. The editor mistook my message and printed the picture along with my last farewell essay, ending the column I had written for 22 years. I was pleased to bid farewell to Mui and my readers with this lovely picture, printed by accident in the newspaper.
- After we had processed a mountain of documents, I was in a bemused state of mind for many hours, only to be calmed by an unexpected spiritual experience in which moments with my dear cats, Mui and Charcoal, came alive as if time had collapsed.
- The memories of my cats calmed me down. Right after that, I met up with another lawyer who was new to us. She gave us some relief by saying that, according to her estimation, our risk was low.
- I hadn't associated Mui with the dream symbol of the lamb, but at the funeral the two appeared to me as a match.

As summarized above, a series of incidents flooded in during the first two weeks of November. The dream, the legal threats, the death of my cat and the timing, and her resemblance to the sacrificial lamb – these are unrelated and a-causal events. But as these unlikely coincidences unfolded in my life, they point to some profound meanings not yet fully known to me.

My daughter instinctively suggested that Mui had sacrificed herself for us. The cat paid the toll so that we could be spared. There is a simple word for that in Chinese: "Deng," meaning to take the blame for a friend. Constance uttered that single word in the middle of it all, "Mui took it for you!" I have that feeling too. A peace offering, a sacrifice to bring peace. A cat protecting her master with her life. A bizarre, superstitious, yet romantic story. I refrain from making such a judgment because there isn't an ounce of empirical evidence for that, no matter how comforting it might sound.

However, some exchanges between the psychosocial and physical are tangible. There is a remarkable resemblance between the lamb (in my dream) and the cat (in reality). My paying tribute to Mui in the sunset coincided with my farewell to my readers. The picture was printed unintentionally – subjective feelings materialized in an unexpected way. I made a strange prayer for the city when I was embodying the lamb in meditation, before the death of my cat. And lastly, in the spiritual experience at the meadowland, the memories of my cats actually calmed my jittery mind, which coincidentally mirrored an unknown lawyer calming me down right afterward.

What I can comprehend is that this sequence of synchronistic events is about suffering and resilience. But what I don't understand is the symbolism of the lamb as an offering, which alludes to the spiritual meanings of sacrifice and atonement, peace and deliverance. Is the suffering of a small group of people a sacrifice for the community at large? In a way, that is true. But what could be achieved by the sacrifice? Would it bring deliverance? Does it do any good? And what is my role in all this? Why was my cat caught up in the middle of it all and why has the symbol of the lamb become the anchor for all of these? Why is her death, an emotionally loaded event in real life, meshing with a sacred symbol in the surreal?

Among Jung's ideas concerning dreams, the most original – and the most controversial – is the connection between dream symbolism and the collective unconscious. He argued that some symbols that appear in the dreams of an individual sometimes are beyond the person's experiences. They could well come from the centuries-old accumulation of myths and tales in various cultural and religious traditions. There are bridges and underpasses between the personal and the collective unconscious. The scarab which appeared in the dream of Jung's patient was a sacred symbol of death and rebirth in Egyptian mythology. The synchronicity she experienced spearheaded a breath of fresh air in her stiffened life, echoing the mythical meaning of this ancient symbol.

The symbol of the lamb is rich in meaning in literature, myths and religion, and is especially prominent in the Judeo-Christian tradition. One may see pureness, humility, and meekness in the animal. Hebrews in Old Testament times would spread the blood of a lamb on the doorframes to keep misfortunes away. The lamb has become one of the most significant symbols in Christianity. Christ, as the sacrificial lamb, was defenseless before lethal threat. His death on the cross is the symbol of human suffering in the most extreme form, and his vulnerability becomes the symbol of strength over evil through the sacrifice of his life. His love and forgiveness become the cornerstones of atonement and deliverance.

The dream has a lot to say about people suffering and collective trauma. Many of us, myself included, feel thrown at the crossroads of our time. There are mounting challenges to be dealt with. K-Town had been an affluent and upwardly mobile society for more than half a century. Its citizens are hardworking and diligent, treasuring materialistic success. However, the city, like many places around the world hard hit by the pandemic and other social upheavals, has started to change at an unthinkably fast rate. What we most need now is not another bucket of gold, but love and care to survive challenges, the resilience to endure, the willingness to share burdens, the tenderness to overcome antagonism, and the hope for a reconciliatory future. In my dream and in my life, a dense web of events evolves around the sacred symbol of the sacrificial lamb. Symbols and events are interrelated yet coincidental, giving me a deep sense of relevance, but I can't yet clearly articulate their meanings and implications in full.

Chapter 3

Reprocessing the Dream of the Moving Stairs

Eye Movement Desensitization and Reprocessing (EMDR)

In 2015, Constance was clinically diagnosed with severe depression, anxiety, and an eating disorder. In addition to receiving professional treatment, she has been working with me to deal with her issues through Focusing and dream analysis. I have read a lot and have participated in workshops on the various ways to treat emotional disorders. In a way, these methods all have a similar emphasis on exploring one's psyche and being sensitive to emerging feelings. Focusing taps into the felt sense of the body, and dreamwork uses the language of the unconscious and other therapeutic methods to get in touch with suppressed traumas, large and small. After a few years of practicing, I now use these methods interchangeably, paying attention to the formation of the felt sense, dream symbolism, inner voices, and patterned reactions.

Of great help has been *The Body Keeps the Score*, written by veteran psychiatrist Bessel van der Kolk who has more than 30 years of experience in treating PTSD. Van der Kolk talks about mindfulness, yoga, and drama therapy, which according to him have longer lasting therapeutic effects than medication. One method that he mentions is "Eye Movement, Desensitization and Reprocessing (EMDR)". At first glance, it seems a playful and frivolous treatment that shouldn't be taken seriously. It involves using a finger or a pointer to lead the eye movement of the patient from left to right and back, repeatedly. By this unlikely action, forgotten details of suppressed trauma will emerge and have a chance to be reprocessed. The fact that a leading expert in the field such as Van der Kolk endorses this treatment roused my curiosity to know more.

The method has been proven useful in clinical research, and for more than 30 years Van der Kolk has used it to treat patients, after trying it himself for the first time in the 1990s. At that time there was a young psychologist in Van der Kolk's therapy group who was addicted to drugs, and frequently fought with her colleagues. She lived a messy life but managed to get her PhD from a prestigious university and was able to start a quite successful career in a care center for abused girls. Van der Kolk witnessed her gradual recovery, not through participation in his group therapy, but by receiving EMDR treatment. That incident motivated Van der Kolk to train in EMDR himself.

In a workshop he was paired up with a partner to go through the drill. As his training partner led him through the eye movement procedure, forgotten childhood memories came back to him: conflicts in the family, fighting at school, etc. And, interestingly, these memories were juxtaposed with a career setback he was facing at the time. A scene came to his mind in which his superior told him to close his clinic at MIT due to a funding shortage. This new wound was overshadowed as old scars emerged. He was aware of this overshadowing – memories were articulated and reprocessed, giving him a sense of relief. Van der Kolk found it inspiring that EMDR is able to loosen the dead knots in our neuro-circuitry, decontextualize traumatic memories, and re-contextualize them into the larger web of life experiences.

EMDR was "discovered" rather randomly. One day in 1987 psychologist Francine Shapiro was out walking in a park when some painful memories surfaced for her. It was by accident, almost, that she noticed that her rapid eye movement could reduce her pain and anxiety. She did some empirical studies to verify her experience and later developed a standardized method of conducting EMDR, which is especially effective in treating PTSD.

Van der Kolk points out that, distinct from anxiety disorder and various kinds of phobia, PTSD originates from real catastrophic threats that re-structure the neuro-circuitry of the trauma survivor, altering his/her self-perception (to being helpless and desperate) and the perception of the outside world (as dangerous and hostile). These fixated neuropathways and somatic chain reactions have to be loosened before the patient can begin to step out of the predicament.

In the weeks following, I immersed myself in books, articles, and demonstration videos to acquire the skills of EMDR, with the hope of trying it out with Constance. We had done a lot of Focusing sessions together and a safety net of trust and rapport had been built between us. She had been seeing her clinical psychologist once a week for almost three years, and every evening after dinner Constance and I would take a walk along the waterfront. We talked about her work, her childhood, and often of her difficult times in high school. The three of us, the psychologist, Constance, and I, all had a general understanding of the traumas she had gone through but there were some blocks in her experience that were completely blank. I hoped EMDR might help her fish out some hints of those forgotten episodes.

Constance's First EMDR Session

On a leisurely Sunday we sat face to face to begin our first EMDR session. At that time, I was not aware of the fact that my lack of professional training would jeopardize the healing process; if forgotten traumatic experiences come back strong, I might not be able to cope. I diligently followed the steps and asked Constance to move her eyes sideways, back and forth. After not too long, large drops of tears rolled down her face. The speed of her response caught me by surprise. I took some deep breaths to ground myself and provided firm support for Constance. She was taking short breaths and her face was flushed. There was something going on, and Constance was totally immersed in herself.

Before trying EMDR we had already located one of her big traumas, which happened in the first year at her new high school. Constance and her classmates, with English as their second language, had been transferred from their local primary school to this international school. They were all assigned to set 5 of the English class except Constance, who was assigned to set 1, the most advanced class. The students there had been at the international school since their primary years. They all knew each other and were fluent in English. They were mostly from super-rich families.

Constance, misplaced to set 1, couldn't understand what the teacher and her classmates were saying in class. The language difficulty and the difference in social class resulted in an unbearable sense of inferiority in her. She resorted to pretending to be asleep during class to avoid being asked questions. She was unable to answer in English. She looked asleep but was fully alert the whole time.

That was all she could remember. No further details. Her memory of the English class for the whole year was a blank. As Van de Kolk said, this prolonged traumatic experience had re-structured her emotive and somatic reactions. Painful feelings had been banished and forgotten; defensive and compensatory measures had been firmly installed.

This EMDR session was the first time Constance had been able to recall some specific images from her blackout class time. The scene returned strongly, vivid and real, blown up into a surreal close-up of the teacher's moustache twitching as he spoke. She couldn't see his face, only his lips and chin. As a dutiful teacher would, he kindly invited Constance to come to the front of the class and give synonyms of a particular word. She was trembling inside but stayed calm on the surface. When the teacher asked other classmates to help, Constance felt ashamed to the core. Abruptly, the scene ended.

The Victim and the Abuser

During the following night Constance had several bad dreams, waking up frequently, sweating all over.

We had another EMDR session the next evening. This time I paid more attention to providing a safe space for Constance before going into the eye movement exercise. The bringing up of suppressed emotions is for desensitizing and re-processing, not merely for re-experiencing the trauma one more time. A safe vantage point in the present moment is essential to facilitate re-processing.

Kathy McGuire, a senior mentor from the International Focusing Institute, teaches an exercise for self-compassion in a guided meditation video, which was originally designed by Pete Campbell and Ed McMahon. I used it as an aid to prepare Constance for her EMDR experience. Following McGuire's instruction, Constance and I closed our eyes, imagined ourselves in an empty hospital, and saw an abandoned baby lying on the floor. McGuire asked us to mobilize our feelings and intention to take care of the baby, and then to take care of ourselves with the same compassion we had for the baby. We were both in deep contemplation and I had a sense that we were sharing the same memory of Charcoal, our beloved cat.

In 2003 we picked up baby Charcoal when he was very sick and feeble inside a cage in a pet shop. In the same cage was a sick dog. I guessed both were about to be euthanized. Constance insisted on taking Charcoal home. We did. Later the vet said Charcoal had FIP, a fatal feline disease at that time, and advised us to have him put to sleep. We didn't. Charcoal survived. We had Charcoal with us for twelve years of loving companionship. He passed away in 2015.

My eyes closed, listening to McGuire's voice, the scene of us picking up Charcoal at the pet shop came up, along with the loving memories of the years we spent together. That was on Constance's mind too, she told me afterward. We, each of us, started the EMDR session with warm feelings and fond memories of Charcoal in our hearts.

Halfway into the eye movement exercise another forgotten scene came up, which surprised both of us. In Constance's flashback, she found herself in the midst of bullying her classmate, M. Both newcomers to the school, M and Constance were treated as oddballs by their classmates, and the two had quickly become buddies. During a school trip to Beijing an arrangement had been made for M to meet the boy she had a crush on in one of the hotel rooms. This was supposed to be a private meeting. Instead, it was a big setup. All the rest of the students were there to humiliate M.

Constance had been asked to set the "joke" up and she had complied. The conflicting emotions concerning her part in this were so overwhelming that they had tangled themselves into a messy blockage, which was sealed up and banished from her consciousness. While the incident itself was completely deep inside, the emotions were still active, and had been all along in the form of self-hatred and self-harming.

Constance experienced these flashbacks during the EMDR without me knowing any of the details. She said a little about some of the scenes in the intervals of the eye movements. When the session was done, I immediately followed it up with another session of Focusing.

At a safe distance I invited Constance to unpack the blockage bit by bit. The complexity of the unfolding emotions amazed me. There were thrills and excitement when Constance witnessed once again the frantic shouting, teasing, and laughing of the crowd which inflicted pain on M. After so many years Constance could still feel the arousal. The drama was "fun" to watch. But shame and guilt immediately rushed in like a big wave. She had betrayed her friend. M left for another school and they have never spoken to each other since.

As Constance looked at this long-forgotten incident in relative calm and from a distance, more delicate emotions became apparent. Behind all the commotion Constance had felt intense fear, the fear of being the next one to be bullied and humiliated in a secret plot against her. Siding with M would have been dangerous. Joining the big group would be safer. It was an improper act taken for her own survival, but she was crushed by the burden of the guilt she had to bear. She couldn't forgive herself for being so cruel and unfaithful to a friend who had trusted her.

At the beginning of *The Body Keeps the Score,* Van der Kolk tells the story of a Vietnam veteran suffering from severe PTSD. He had witnessed the brutal deaths of his comrades, but a major part of his PTSD was the haunting memory of his having killed some innocent Vietnamese kids in revenge. He was the victim of an enormous trauma; he was also the abuser. To get in touch with himself again he had to face his memories and learn to forgive.

In a similar vein, Constance's blockage had to be unpacked to allow more space for her to re-experience the contradictory emotions embedded in her memory. Looking back, she could have walked away and refused to take part in the bullying – and would choose to do that if she had the chance to make the choice again. But she understood that at that time she was too overwhelmed by fear. This reprocessing would allow her to have more compassion and empathy for the twelve-year-old Constance.

I consulted Dr. Eddie Chiu, a good friend of mine and a veteran clinical psychologist, about the EMDR sessions that I did with Constance. His advice was that it is not safe for me to do it, better ask a specialist if Constance wants to have another round of EMDR. I think I was not sensitive enough before. I took his advice and decided not to conduct EMDR myself.

She had lots of dreams in the following weeks. My hunch was that, as suppressed memories loosened up after a few sessions of EMDR, so too did other entangled experiences from deep in her unconscious start to come to the surface in her dreams. The dreams were invitations for Constance to go deeper into the reprocessing of her perception about her past and herself.

Dreamwork: Bias Control

There is a popular perception that a specialized psychologist, a knowledgeable expert, or an experienced mystic can decipher the enigma of a dream. However, in the dream community this popular idea of dream interpretation by an authority figure is considered counterproductive at best and misleading at worst. Dreams are deeply embedded in the psyche of the dreamer. The same dream symbol might have opposite meanings for different individuals. For instance, a dying father in the dream of a submissive man may be the expression of his suppressed desire to walk away from the shadow of his father. But for a caring and assertive son, the same dream scene may be a straightforward expression of his anxiety over his father's deteriorating health. Dreamers have to work on their own dreams to attain a deeper self-understanding. As Louis Savary et al. write in *Dreams and Spiritual Growth*, "dreamwork is like opening the letter, reading it, and responding to it."

After Constance's EMDR experiences, she had a series of vivid dreams that begged for some serious dreamwork. The first perplexing dream symbol was a moving staircase.

In the dream, Constance comes back home and finds that there is a birthday party taking place in our lobby, in the middle-class estate we have been living in for some 20 years. This fancy party, held by a few rich moms for their elaborately dressed kids, is in big contrast to the plain décor of the venue.

Constance has to walk past those fancy balloons and birthday presents to get to the elevator. Camera flashes and cheering sounds make her very uncomfortable. Then she sees the entrance to the back stairs, which is bizarrely ornamented with precious stones. It looks like the grand staircase of a palace.

Constance decides to take the stairs instead of the elevator but her bag becomes bigger and heavier, and the staircase becomes narrower as she strives to walk up. She senses danger, exits the stairs, and takes the elevator again to get back home.

The dream was rich in details. I broke it down into two workable components, the birthday party and the stairs. We worked on the party scene first.

I invited Constance to mindfully go back to the lobby and let the sensations in the dream emerge again. It was like doing Gendlin's Focusing, quietly waiting for the felt sense to reveal itself.

Obviously, she was disturbing the birthday party when she walked past the crowd. The moms and kids had to stop posing for their photoshoot and make way for her. As Constance sensed into the feeling, it was more than simple uneasiness. There was embarrassment and even deep-seated shame behind the hectic rush.

The EMDR experience had had a loosening up effect on Constance. She could now reach deep into her memory and locate similar sensations in the past much more easily than before.

Passing through the dream party felt like an occasion in her 12th grade, where a rich classmate had insisted on taking Constance home. After a few games at the bowling hall away from school, the boy wanted to give Constance a ride home. At the roadside his liveried driver was waiting. Constance didn't have a good excuse to refuse the offer, so she got into the car and felt anxious throughout the ride. Anxiety became intense fear as the car approached home. She asked the driver to let her off at a shopping mall, saying that she had to go to the grocery store. She had kept where she lived a secret because she felt ashamed of her humble home.

It seemed that shame and fear had been locked up for many years and kept emerging in her dreams. The birthday party in the lobby embodied her long-standing shame. Now, in the dream, her rich classmates were right on the doorstep of her humble home.

I asked Constance to identify the differences in the old situation when she was a newbie in a rich kid school and now, years later, when she has "normal" friends, a good job, and a decent home. Re-examining the dream she found that shame and fear were still present, but they seemed to be from an ancient place and were losing their gripping power.

In his book *Let Your Body Interpret Your Dreams*, Gendlin applies his method of Focusing to dreams. Basically his approach has two stages, the first is "to know with bodily sureness what most of your dreams are about". People know about dreams from Freudian, Jungian or some other viewpoints, which might give us a cognitive "aha", and make a plausible "fit". But Gendlin asks us to approach the dream, not with any conceptual lens, but by felt-sensing the touchstone inside of us that is the somatic sensation the dream carries. "When the felt sense of the dream opens in their bodies, they won't need anyone to convince them." That's why Gendlin stressed, "Only the dreamer's body can interpret the dream."

The second stage is about getting something new from the dream. Stage one (felt sensing) and two (getting something new) often come together – when you touch the touchstone, so to speak, it may also come with a shift, which brings a step of personal growth. But sometimes a felt shift tells what the dream is about – and yet brings nothing new for the dreamer that isn't already known in waking life. In that case, the dreamer needs to go for stage two, to get something new, to find a growth-direction and move forward.

Gendlin's advice is to approach our inward sensation in a friendly way. Wait for the felt sense to come. "To let it come, first sense the middle of the body from inside. Then think of a problem, or some part of the dream."

A felt sense is not just an emotion that you can label. It is different, it is fuzzy, evolving, not clearly known at first. You have to be patient. "It is a bodily quality, like *heavy, sticky, jumpy, fluttery, tight*. At first it has no fitting label." When it comes, it gives you the energy to move forward. It is expansive, life-enhancing.

Gendlin gives us some concrete tools to help us open up our dreams and allow something new to come. He calls it "Bias Control" – to soften our bias towards the familiar path we have strolled umpteen times. You can either get into the villain/negative character in your dream, play it out and sense its perspective of looking at the dream world, or you can get into your dream ego (the me in the dream), but take the opposite attitude or values, especially when your dream ego is acting in a way that is familiar in your waking life. Some guiding questions might be: Is what you say about the dream something you usually say? Are you expressing your usual feelings and values? If so, what would be the opposite feelings and values?

There is no need to adopt or reject the opposite interpretation. Bias control is there to open up the familiar, to allow something new to have space to emerge.

Back to Constance's party dream. She spent some time at stage one and found an age-old sensation of fear and shame with a bodily sureness. The dream came about as she "unearthed" the forbidden memories of her high school traumas in the EMDR sessions. Shame and fear remained active but the specifics had gone, had been obliterated. But as Gendlin points out, those things have already been there for a long time. What is new? What could be done? How to move forward?

Well, dissociating shame and fear from the past with her present situation already pointed to a growth-direction. And in fact, her reaction in the dream was very typical of her. "The fault is mine", as always. This is her first reaction to any blameworthy situation in life. She is hard on herself.

This time, I asked her to try out bias control, felt-sensing the dream from a completely opposite perspective, imagining making judgments and reactions directly opposite to those of her dream ego.

She paused for a while, then spoke softly to herself. "It isn't my fault. I'm not trespassing. In fact, it is the rich moms organizing their fancy party in the wrong place. They are disturbing us residents and blocking the way to the elevator. A residential lobby is a big mismatch for their extravagant display."

I asked how she felt, comparing the felt sense of her shame narrative against the rich moms being at fault narrative. When she adopted "the fault is mine" attitude of her dream ego (as well as of her waking self), she found "it constricts. You get tight, smaller. You breathe less. You get cramped. You wilt."

When she made the judgment that the rich moms' party shouldn't have been held in the lobby, she had the feeling of what Gendlin says in his book: "You expand, you are more, the energy flows from inside you outward."

In her active imagination, she stepped up and told the party moms that it was not good to block the lobby, they would be much happier partying at the nearby park by the seaside. She told me that in her imagination she had Mui with her, our cat who was scared by strangers. "Look, you are upsetting my poor cat!" Constance held her hands forward, as if she was holding the cat in the faces of the rich moms, who felt embarrassed. Constance chuckled. The turnaround had been achieved.

Contrary to common belief, dreams are not self-contained. Their symbols can be brought to our daily routines to achieve personal growth. They can have a "life" outside the dream. They can move us forward in our waking life.

Dreamwork: Symbol Immersion

For the second part of Constance's dream, the ornamented staircase full of glittery symbols, I found the technique of "symbol immersion" in Louis Savary's book quite useful. The procedure is as follows:

- "...select an image or symbol from the dream which attracts you, which seems vivid, and of which you would like to be more aware."
- "In your imagination, let your dream come alive again and focus on your chosen symbol. Keep the symbol in the state it was in the original dream..."
- "Relate to your symbol in any way that makes it more vivid and important to you. For example, in imagination change your position in order to perceive the symbol in greater detail..."
- "If you are with a dream partner or in a dream group, let them ask questions that will make the symbol clearer to you..."

Constance said the symbols of the staircase which stood out to her were the marble steps, the gems, the crystal chandelier, the grand entrance, and the narrowing space. All were disorienting and puzzling. I asked her to use the techniques of Focusing: grounding, felt-sensing, being mindful of the emerging emotions.

After a while, Constance selected the image of the railing on the wall as a focus for her attention. She started with the sensation of holding the bronze rail, which was golden in color and finely engraved. Details gradually came forth. The rail was inlaid with ivory white opals, lucent and smooth. In the dream, Constance had held the rail for balance, now she recognized an insecure feeling. To her surprise the staircase was in fact moving, narrowing, as if it was a sentient being with the ill-intent of sucking her up into the far end of the stairs.

There is another follow-up technique in Savary's book that can be applied here – the technique of Carrying the Symbol Forward:

- "...re-enter the dream and focus on the symbol. The symbol may spontaneously change or act in such a way that it proceeds forward in time. If the symbol doesn't do this automatically, you may invite it to do so..."
- "Once the symbol begins to move forward in time, simply follow its change or movement. Notice how the symbol relates to you and how you relate to the symbol..."
- "When the procedure comes to a natural stopping place... reflect on the process, asking yourself questions such as: What have I learned about the symbol? ... What energies, feelings or insights have been released in me..."

In the dream, Constance didn't stay on the staircase for very long but, following the steps suggested above, the process slowly took some new twists and turns not experienced in the dream. With one hand holding the rail and the other carrying a heavy bag, she found it difficult to keep her balance because the stairs started meandering as if there was, as she put it, something sneaky, about to devour her in the shrinking space.

Holding onto the rail bought her some time to be mindful of the emotional changes. She had been attracted into the stairway by the grand and luxurious entrance, eye-pleasing and fascinating. But now she felt the alertness of imminent danger. She sensed some kind of a "will" hidden at the far end of the shrinking space, like a force which was about to suck her in. At that moment, she decided to exit the stairs and head for the elevator, which at once rendered the elevator lobby plain and normal again.

As to the question of the lesson the dream might be offering her, Constance had no idea. She could find no association with or insight into anything in her waking life – at least, not until a few days later when she had another dream, after which the meaning of the shrinking staircase naturally presented itself to her mind.

The Pet Frog Dream

In this new dream, Constance is living with a few dozen friends in a community court. There are rival factions competing for popularity in this nest of intrigue. Constance has a tiny tree frog as a pet in her front pocket. She doesn't know how to take care of the frog, but a friendly girl who is experienced in keeping a pet frog is willing to teach her what to do. However, she is from the opposing camp and their getting together might breed suspicion and speculation.

Suddenly a huge tsunami closes in from all sides. There is no escape. Constance doesn't want to die inside the enclosed building. She jumps out of the window to the open sea with the frog in her pocket. She wakes up.

We did the usual dreamwork of re-experiencing the scenes. I asked Constance to extend the timing of her flashback, so that she could slowly discern the minute changes of mood and feelings. I was amazed by how many details she could recall: the eerie scraping noises when the waves washed against the walls, the misty gusts of wind battering her face, the smell of the salty sea, the gradually intensifying anxiety.

Suddenly, in a flash, she had a strong recollection of what was in her mind when she decided to jump: the wheeling and dealing, the popularity contest, secret intrigues, who's who in rival groups – these things didn't matter anymore. Jumping out of the window, even if she died, was a much better option than dying in the company of a bunch of manipulative friends and foes.

In high school, she was introduced to luxurious labels, vintage wines, collectable watches, high table manners. She learned by heart all these cultural assets. She was eager to compete with her classmates. Nevertheless, for her, their luxurious lifestyles were unattainable and unaffordable no matter how hard she tried.

Added to this was the complication that most of her rich classmates were nice to her. Sure, they were condescending, but most of them had taken care of her, especially with regard to her share of their entertainment bills. She did not have to pay most of the time. She aspired to be one of them but couldn't. The friends in her communal living dream all came out of twisted memories in her unconscious mind.

This new dream let her make sense of the moving staircase in the previous dream. The symbol of the devouring staircase in the lobby party dream became clearer when she juxtaposed it with the pet frog dream. She realized that the luxuriously ornamented staircase represented her desire to blend into the circle of her rich classmates, which had been detrimental to her psychological health. Her insight in the dream – *it doesn't matter anymore* – freed her from the bondage of endless competition for popularity and wealth. To avoid a danger she couldn't foresee, she left the staircase in the previous dream. In this new dream, jumping out of the window was a much bolder and more radical way to leave the rat race behind.

One mystery of the dream remained to be deciphered: the pet frog. Constance tried again with symbol immersion and carrying forward. When she mindfully tended to the image of the frog, she could feel its fragility. It had, in fact, only the faintest breath of life left at the start since Constance didn't know how to take care of it. Having learned from the frog expert friend, her pet gradually gathered some strength, its skin becoming moistly translucent and whitish yellow in color. The tiny fingers of its front limbs stuck out of Constance's pocket.

The frog was settled and calm. Its peace of mind was in big contrast to the trickeries of the boys and girls in the commune.

I asked Constance the questions in Savary's tool book: "The dream ends when you jump out of the window with the frog in your pocket so what happens next? If you let the dream move forward, what would the resolution be? And what about the frog?"

It only took a few seconds for a new scene to appear in Constance's mind: she and the frog landed on a huge lily pad floating on the high sea. She looked carefully at the frog, which sat on its new home and was completely at ease. Despite its soft and tiny build, the frog was full of life. There was a naïve liveliness on its face. The sea in front of them was vast and there was a bit of excited expectation in Constance's mind to see what life would be like on the lily pad.

Constance commented that it was strange to have such an intimate attachment to a pet frog in her dream because she doesn't like watching wildlife documentaries. She hates frogs. She finds them repulsive. On one or two occasions she has seen frogs kept in cages for sale in the wet market. Frog dishes appear on Chinese menus. They are edible, and available in the market alive – dirty green in color with rough spotty skin. The very sight of them makes Constance shiver. So the question was, how come the frog symbol, so foreign to Constance's life, found its way into her dream?

I have read Jung's writings on archetypal symbols, which trickle, he claimed, from the collective unconscious down to individual dreams. It is difficult for me to subscribe to this mystical phenomenon - how can a symbol unknown to a dreamer be of meaning to him or her?

However, Constance's pet frog is such a connection between the personal and the mythical. I was surprised to find that the frog is an ancient Egyptian symbol for fertility, rebirth, and transformation. The annual flooding of the Nile was the breeding ground for frogs, bringing fertility to the land when the water receded. In Constance's dream, instead of a flooding there was a huge tsunami. The frog got in, which signified a noteworthy turning point in the predicament of her dream as well as in her recovery in waking life.

She had made sense of the moving staircase, the commune and the pet frog. The frog, for Constance, was a sign of transformation. That was the meaning that unfolded at that point.

The Precognition of the Mythic Frog

To the surprise of the whole family, the pet frog was more than that. Two months after the dream, completely out of the blue, Constance's menstruation came back. It had totally stopped for seven years, yet all of a sudden it began again, not intermittently, but regularly once a month.

It is not uncommon for patients suffering from an eating disorder to have menstrual irregularities. A pause of one or two years and then beginning again is not uncommon, but after seven years it is not likely to come back. We, along with her doctors and her nutritionist, had already considered her menopause as permanent.

During the beginning of her seven years of presumed menopause, Constance had tried various methods to restore her periods. Hormone tests indicated a low score of close to zero. Pushing up the hormonal level by taking contraceptive pills pumped her body up, which she abhorred. She also tried a few alternative options, including taking daily herbal medicine for a whole year.

Once a week we visited a renowned Chinese herbal medicine master, famed for healing some bigshots in town. Each round trip involved an hour of driving and another hour spent waiting for the assistant to pick and precisely weigh the dry ingredients of the herbal medicine for the whole week. It was a test of willpower and discipline. Every day I had to use a pressure cooker to boil a bowl of murky liquid for Constance to drink. I had to pay extra attention to the timing of the preparation because, according to the master, the healing effect might be adversely affected if I messed up the delicate balance between the opposing ingredients. A particular ingredient would turn bad if overcooked. Our endurance was tested to the limit.

The master had complete confidence in restoring Constance's menstruation. He told Constance not to wear shorts, to keep her legs warm, to soak her feet in warm water before bed. She had to eat different restorative dishes in different seasons, like lamb casserole in the winter for instance. He even predicted the timing of the return of her menstruation. High hopes, big disappointment. The famous herbal master failed to deliver on his promise. This was just one instance of several vicious cycles of expectation and frustration.

As Constance's emotions had become stable, with no more life-threatening suicidal impulses, we had accepted the fact that she was already in menopause at the exceptionally early age of her 20s. It was not going to come back. As long as she had the stamina to get on with her life, having periods or not was not an issue to any of us. And suddenly, Aunty M visited her again (a Chinese euphemism for menstruation), and Aunty M is here to stay.

There was no forewarning, except for the frog in her dream, the full meaning of which we hadn't grasped at once. After seven years of going from disappointment to no hope at all, suddenly it returned. This is nothing short of a small miracle.

I googled the frog symbol again. In Egyptian mythology, Heqet is the frog-goddess of fertility. She is believed to hold power over the baby's body and life in the womb, and the safety of both mother and child during labor and delivery.

I am amazed at the matching of the mythic, the personal, the psychic and the actual happenings in her dreams and her waking life.

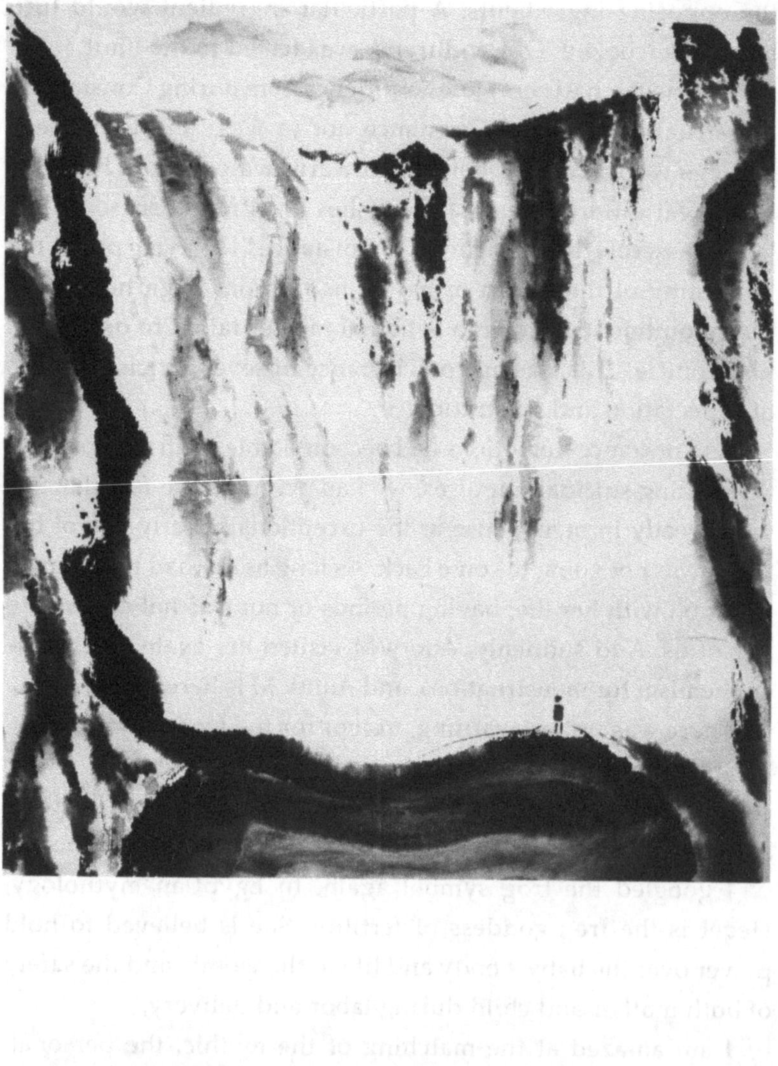

Chapter 4

The Sublime Moment of the I Ching Oracle

The Travel Plan

I hadn't contemplated leaving the city but my friends urged me to leave. For the first time, I had a wish to start a new life elsewhere. Leaving would be difficult. Aside from my strong sense of belonging to the city, my major concern was for Constance's psychological health. She was steadily recovering, had a stable and rewarding job, a nice boyfriend, and a comfort zone where she felt safe and secure. Teresa and I had accompanied her through her difficult times. Our leaving would rock her boat too much. If she left with us she would have to leave her job and her boyfriend, Fred, behind. He has been very supportive as, little by little, Constance shared the dark side of her life with him. Fred would not be able to leave as he cared for his father who has a chronic illness. Emigrating to another country was a very difficult move for all of us.

That day, Teresa and I went hiking with Kenny and his wife Valerie. We have been traveling partners since 2017. During lunch at a villa-turned-teahouse in the countryside, Valerie asked whether we would entertain the idea of taking a trip to Australia. The COVID-19 Pandemic had prevented most K-Town citizens from traveling because of strict quarantine measures. We hadn't been to the airport for almost two years.

I made a quick decision to go with them – not to leave K-Town for good, but to test the water to see whether I could leave without hindrance. Staying away from worries for a few months would be good. Besides, we could check out what life was like for our emigrant friends in Australia. After the decision had been made, I felt quite relieved, as if a heavy burden had been taken from my shoulders.

Teresa and Valerie spent quite some time planning the long trip. We intended to stay in Australia for a month, then have another 3 weeks in Canada. Car rentals, hotel arrangements, plane tickets etc. were all a bit complicated. Since these were the two favorite destinations of the many K-Town citizens who chose to emigrate, prices were soaring and accommodations were not easy to secure.

Our plan to travel shocked Constance, and she was smart enough to know there was the suggestion behind it of us leaving K-Town for good. She was quick to say that she would choose to be with us no matter where we planned to go. Fred would have to stay in K-Town to take care of his father. Between us and Fred, she'd choose to leave with us.

Fred joined the three of us for a half-day trip to the outer island of Penguin Bay. On the ferry, I struggled to write messages to my lawyer Mr. T and to the other lawyer, Mandy, who viewed my case quite differently. She was generous in offering help in those anxious days, while Mr. T was officially my lawyer hired by Neil, the company secretary. I wanted to inform them of my travel plan. I ought to have sent the messages earlier, but there was something in my chest, heavy and unpleasant, which prevented me from asking the lawyers directly about my chances of leaving. My procrastination was a sign of my anxiety. I guess I was afraid of the reply I might get. It wasn't until the ferry had docked at the pier that I finally gathered my strength to press the send button.

Penguin Bay is peaceful and lovely, with little cottages scattered along the seaside and up into the small hills. We ordered some dim sum and shared lunch on a bench by the sea. Afterward we took a walk up the hill and I had some time alone with Fred to tell him of my situation and of our plans for travel. Our talk was pleasant but we were unused to each other. This was the first time he'd heard the details from me. He was calm and said he would take care of Constance while we were away.

As Constance had been under our all-encompassing care for the past seven years it was a relief to know there was someone close to her willing to take on that responsibility. Nevertheless, I couldn't feel certain. Fred, for me, was a new acquaintance. I didn't know much about him.

Mandy replied that afternoon, saying that it would be safe for me to leave town. I was relieved to hear that. An hour later, Mr. T called. His advice was more constrained, saying that my leaving might alert the stakeholders and, in his estimation, I'd have a 20% chance of being targeted, preempting my leaving. They knew my whereabouts and might already be watching my movements. I understood this difference to come from the fact that Mandy was a friend, and T was officially my lawyer, who had a duty to protect himself and prepare me for the worst scenario. Despite the gentle warning from T, I took it as a green light for me to go ahead with my travel plan.

Back at home, Constance told me that Fred had been surprised that Teresa was so calm at lunch as we talked about the challenge our family was facing. If I ended up in trouble, the burden of taking care of the family would fall on her shoulders. Teresa is stable, at ease, and full of confidence. Although we no longer went to church, she is still a faithful Christian. It's not that she was sure of my safety, but she seemed to have faith in our ability to face adversity together. She is extraordinarily brave and courageous. Instead of needing any support from me, she actually calmed me down by asking me to follow divine guidance rather than wavering with the conflicting advice from friends and lawyers. She is a blessing, as always. She makes our home safe and full of love.

Dream of the Caught-up Cat

As we were busily planning our two-month tour, I had a pretty obvious dream about an escape:

I am staying in a big hotel room somewhere in Europe. Our plan is to stay there for two weeks then head for Paris. Suddenly I receive a message: not safe here, schedule has to be changed, need to leave immediately. I pack my stuff in great haste. It is messy. There's too much to carry, the bags are too small. I have two cats, where can I get a cat carrier to put them in?

I decided to take Mui with me and leave the other cat with a friend. Mui is hidden inside a foldable luggage bag, but she pushes through the zip and dashes out – except that one of her front legs gets caught in a strap outside the bag. The more she struggles, the tighter the grip. I calm her down, set her paw free. She sits tight on the bag. I wake up.

Obviously, the dream reflected my anxiety. In the evening, I arranged a dream workshop via Zoom. Our teacher, Ed, was curious about the front leg of the cat being caught in the fold of a strap. He even used his left hand to hold his right wrist, asking, "How does it feel?" I intuitively thought of handcuffs, but I avoided answering the question. I said with confidence, "The cat is calm. I calmed her down." Then I described my felt sense of the fat cat sitting tight there. She was heavy, full of energy.

I was aware of my skillful manipulation of the dream to fit my wish. I wanted to go ahead with my travel plans and didn't want to acknowledge any warning from a dream. It is not the meaning of the dream that's worth recording here, but the malleability of its interpretation in favor of my preference and of what I wanted to avoid. I didn't want the dream to be read as apprehension of my being handcuffed, so I actively introduced a tangible sensation of my fat cat staying put – her massive body could be felt at my arm. I took it as a reminder to be unflustered under pressure. The felt sense of me being handcuffed was unmistakably there, only I chose to ignore it.

***

(Here is a brief note from Dec 29, 2022, after proofreading the draft paragraphs above, written earlier that year. The meaning of the dream became much clearer as I read the draft again. Mui, the cat in the dream, was in fact me, eager to get out. The dream was a reflection of my anxiety over what would happen, and what, it turned out, almost did happen: Candice, in her divination, advised me not to leave the city, otherwise there would be misfortune. See page 81. The alert came twice. The dream came out of my own apprehension, while the divination was a warning. In the end, I stayed put, like the cat in the dream.)

Self-Care in Nature

Brian had taken a course entitled *Self-care in Nature* and recommended it to me. Some years ago, another friend had told me about the same course. He had stayed in the woods for a week and learned to communicate with trees. I was skeptical. It sounded odd to be talking to trees.

What made me decide to join this time was Kenny. He was sick and he loves trees. In just a few months his panic attacks had become much more frequent. Some time ago he started a project of matching small branches to handmade pottery, with the aim of inviting people to appreciate the beauty of trees. I asked Kenny to come on the course with me. There were four day trips in two weekends and some Zoom classes in between. A few days in the countryside might help ease his anxiety.

The first day of the course began with a Zoom session with Clara, our teacher in France. For the past 15 years she had come every year to K-Town to lead this self-care program at Karrie Farm. Because of the COVID pandemic she couldn't conduct the course in person, so we Zoomed.

She asked us to close our eyes and imagine what we were expecting to experience in the coming two weeks. Following her guidance, I recalled some of my recent synchronistic experiences. There seemed to be unexplained connections between myself and the flow of life. I called it the in-between space, which can be felt but can't be explained in rational terms. It is like a web of ties between the conscious mind and the oneness of all things. I closed my eyes, and tried to visualize this in-between space and, in my mind, there was this ethereal aura, light purple and blue, flowing slowly. It was vivid – but I guessed it could just be my active imagination.

After the Zoom session, our tutor Annie took us out to open ground beside a confluence of streams. She said, "For most people, when they hike, their aim is *getting somewhere*. But *being here* is good enough." She invited us to be more aware of the sound, smell, and ambiance of the nature we were in.

There we were, in an open area surrounded by shrubs and loose clumps of trees, layer upon layer, stretching afar. I found a comfortable spot by the stream, closed my eyes, and remained alert. We were used to being in the countryside as outsiders, appreciating the wonders of nature, relaxing ourselves. Annie reminded us that we are part of nature, embedded from within, not watching from without.

In this way, I submerged myself in the soundscape of running waters, singing birds, and leaves whispering in the gentle breezes. The air was forest-like with the scent of green and moisture all over. I followed Annie's guided meditation and started to breathe in the gifts of nature and breathe out my worries and concerns. I was grateful to feel welcome as part of this lively habitat, and the immense space before me was more than enough to keep thoughts of my predicament at bay. I felt supported by a woodland that was welcoming and generous. There was an in-between space between me, the trees, the running waters, and the singing birds. We are connected in mysterious ways which can be felt intuitively when our heart is open and our mind clear.

One classmate recalled some verses from the Chinese philosopher Zhuangzi – Nature doesn't talk about its majestic beauty, nor its rhythm of the coming and going of seasons. The more I looked deeply into the beauty around me, the more I appreciated the wisdom of Zhuangzi. Nature doesn't say much in our usual language. Heaven and earth are no anxious preachers – no convincing is necessary. The rhythm of seasons, the blossoming and withering of life, the bursting colors of birds, butterflies, and flowers, all these wonders are in the eyes of the beholder.

You Are All Around Me

I was in a barber shop when a text came from Mandy. It was an update telling me that the managing executive of the company was being interrogated and charges were being pressed. It was late afternoon. As I headed home, fear shot through my chest.

In the Zoom meeting with Clara and the group that evening I was all over the place. Messages kept coming in asking about my safety. I couldn't stay focused on the Zoom screen. Just reading the messages on my phone set me on edge. A senior accountant was being interrogated as I was attending the meeting.

My daughter came home from work and I left the study to say hello to her. I looked into her eyes, hugged her, and whispered, "We are facing big dangers and grave difficulties ahead. Together we can stay strong."

I returned to my Zoom class, my mind mostly blank for the first hour. During the break, I found a handwritten card on the table. My daughter had left me a note and gone for a walk along the waterfront.

"Unable to perceive the shape of you, I find you all around me. Your presence fills my heart, for you are everywhere."

It is a quote from the poem at the end of the movie *The Shape of Water*. She had added, "You are the air we breathe, for me, for mum, for Mui, and Charcoal."

Throughout the years of Constance's long history of depression and eating disorders I had been her carer, and here, in the middle of this storm, she was my strength. Those words she wrote were magical, casting a safety net all around me.

Back in my Zoom class, when Clara talked about trees it made perfect sense. Trees, as well as being part of nature, are a channel of energy. They are not judgmental. They help each other out. Connecting with trees brings us wellbeing, calmness, and compassion. With what Constance had written and with Clara's teaching I found my anchor again.

An Invitation from the Companion Tree

Brian said his clever friend Candice had made a divination for both of us, and he wanted to discuss it in person. So we met at a Chinese teahouse.

I was anxious about the outcome. The reading wasn't bad. It said I would be ok despite some disturbances. It specifically advised me to stay with the group, not to venture out alone.

At that time Candice didn't know me. She asked Brian whether my daughter was about to get married, because the reading indicated it. Brian said no.

He relayed Candice's comments to me: The script said someone would bother you a bit, but it was going to be a very slow process. There would be a long wait.

I wanted to talk to Candice directly, to fill in the details about my daughter so that we could clear up my confusion and better interpret the I Ching script. I told myself that I shouldn't invest too much in this kind of mysticism but, in a stressful time like this, a coded message from the beyond might keep me afloat.

I stayed up late, alone in the living room with all the lights off. Mind unsettled, heart filled with worries, I was restless. Inside me were butterflies beating their wings in silence. Then I remembered that Clara had asked us to find a companion tree nearby and connect with it.

"That tree in front of our balcony, how about giving it a try?" I said to myself. It was a *Flame of the Forest* which at that time of year was blossoming in ferocious red. But it was dark outside. I could only imagine the shape of its spreading branches and bursting flowers. For the past decade, I have watched this tree grow to a dozen meters high. I looked into the dark, imagining how deep the roots would be, and I could feel the steadfastness it commanded to withstand the winds and rain throughout the years. I recalled my selfish and devilish past wish that a typhoon would uproot it – at that time its big canopy was just at the height of my balcony and it blocked the sea view for quite a few years. I hated the wall of green just outside my window. My eyes yearned for an open view and my frustration turned into hostility. Trees were dispensable. They were objects having value only if they served a function to men.

However, the irony is that the tree has now grown taller and the view outside the balcony is much more picturesque. Now we can see the tides come in and recede under its shade. When I recalled this little secret, I felt ashamed to have had such a self-centered mind-set. I was deeply sorry about my earlier, persistent death wish for the tree. But trees are here – live and let live. They don't discriminate.

I opened the balcony door and took a closer look at the tree. It was veiled in shadowy darkness, but in the faint light coming from my neighbor's window I could see its branches extending towards me, like a pair of welcoming arms inviting me to its mysterious embrace.

Our trip to Australia had almost been finalized. I summoned up the courage to call Valerie to tell her for the first time, and in detail, that I was facing grave danger. Teresa and I couldn't leave the city. She responded with a quick yes and was more than willing to do the cancellation and re-scheduling. The plane tickets had been issued and couldn't be refunded. I knew this was difficult for them. In our previous trips I had shared the driving and now Kenny, with his medical condition, couldn't drive. I was meant to have taken on the driving for our planned trip and my pulling out now caused them some trouble. All four of us, one way or the other, were facing different life challenges and I knew for sure that they would accommodate our last minute pull-out with sympathetic understanding.

In the late afternoon, I decided to spend some time with my newly found companion tree. Under its shade, I sat on a folding chair and paid careful attention to the surroundings. I looked at its roots stretching out and then disappearing into the ground, giving me a sense of stability. Looking up from the base of the tree, I was amazed to see the branches and leaves fanning out all over the canopy, patterned beautifully in a kaleidoscopic array. Red flowers were blossoming. Some had already withered and were slowly falling, petals in yellowish red were sprinkled on this small patch of grass where I was sitting. I wondered, was the tree a poet? It seemed like he was writing his poem with feather-like petals in vertical lines descending from the sky.

Sitting here a bit longer, I slowly recognized that there were ants, bees, small beetles, birds – all co-existing in this tiny cosmos. And gradually the outsider in me began to feel like a member of this micro-life world, comfortably connected. The Flame of the Forest had sustained a network, a friendly alliance of beings living here for nearly two decades. My home was nested in this lively retreat, previously all unknown to me.

A New Assessment

It was a Saturday, and PH and Annie, the two local tutors of the self-care program, took us to Tate Park, a small and peaceful garden with lots of giant trees. They invited us to find a spot, a tree or a scene that would have meaning for us personally. A remote cottage hiding on the side of a distant hill attracted my attention. It stood alone amid the lavish green. The misty atmosphere was heavenly. A soothing thought came to my mind, recalling Constance's handwritten verses: "Your presence fills my heart, for you are all around me, you are everywhere."

The stand-alone building enveloped by trees and thickets, for me, was a symbol of nature's providence.

I had an appointment with Mandy the lawyer in the afternoon, so I had to leave the group. Brian joined us and the three of us met in a safe place in town. Mandy's assessment of my leaving K-Town had changed with the latest development. The chance of me leaving safely now seemed a bit "slim," she said, with uncertainty in her voice. Not quite giving a specific assessment, she instead focused on briefing us about the possible scenarios. All the indirect hints suggested that the threat to us was higher than before, and this made Brian and me quite anxious.

By midnight, I received a message from Brian, relaying some advice from two big shots, that according to their estimation we were on the hit list for sure. Leaving the city might trigger a pre-emptive arrest, but there was still a chance of a narrow escape. It was worth the gamble, they said. This message stirred up big fear, and my mind was firing with thoughts of various exit plans and the traumatic experiences that would arise from these imagined scenarios. Even if I could have a narrow escape, I would then become an exile and could never come back home. At that point, I couldn't reconcile the psychological impact of me leaving for good and the spiritual experience I had just had in the past week. Two extremes. One of tranquility, the other of trepidation.

The Sublime Moment of Grace

In the last field trip of the self-care program, we gathered inside a small house in the morning. PH began the day by asking us to imagine a flower blossoming, revealing its beauty before our eyes. I guessed she was hoping that we might see the positive side no matter what happened to us. It was difficult for me to think of a flower when danger loomed large. Struggling to stay calm, I waited as an image started to unveil itself. It was the image of the withering red flowers of my newly found companion tree outside my balcony. The blossoming period was over and red petals fell like rain when the breeze caught them. I realized that I had never treated the tree as a companion nor a friend. Now when I looked deeply into its graceful manifestation I could see its beauty and wisdom; the leaves drop in the winter leaving only bare branches, then new leaves come freshly in spring, rejuvenating. Next, flowers blossom like fire in summer, and the cycle of life keeps wheeling on.

The tree has been our companion for almost twenty years, witnessing the ups and downs of our family, and showing us its vitality and beauty year after year. When I sit under its shade, I have a warm feeling of being taken care of. It is part of the greater good, protecting our home and guiding our family. The realization that my home is a loving home as well as a spiritual home gives me strength to face the challenge at hand. Before, I loved my home for its physical comfort. I still do, but now my home is more. It is a refuge, a cradle, and a prayer room, giving me strength to resist and endure.

After lunch, when the sky cleared up, we prepared for the main activity of the day – visiting the old camphor tree which stood at the back of the village. We walked past the cottages along a narrow footpath and around the corner, and there it was. This tree surprised us with the gigantic size of its trunk. The canopy was huge, rising a dozen meters above ground. I wondered how many liters of water in any given second were being pumped up from the soil to the branches and leaves above. I couldn't find words to describe the distinct sense of energy flow in the air. The energy was definitely here.

PH invited us to find a stable footing, stand up straight and visualize roots growing from our legs into the soil, reaching far below and connecting with the dense roots of the camphor tree. I tried to open my heart and suspend my disbelief. Much sooner than I thought, I sensed a pull on my leg, and the sensation of heat arose gently from my lower limbs. It was not the one-sided sensation of heat from sunlight, but a saturated feeling of warmth slowly rising to my back and shoulders. My fingers were tingling, and then both arms seemed to flicker and spark.

When PH invited us to let the cosmic energy flow through our body from the head, I felt nothing. "Is this a make-believe fantasy?" I tried to let my experience speak for itself. Surely, I could differentiate the energy from the soil, which was more "saturated," and energy from the sky, which was light and translucent. Amid the flow of these energies my heart was in a peaceful space, light as a feather, clear, and transparent... There, I had no ego, nor a "me". I related to the trees, the grassy soil, the singing birds, to the friends standing by my side. I was part of the whole, but I still had a self, a being beyond the framing of time. Then came gentle breezes, as if the giant tree was talking to me in the language of silence. Time stood still. Full of peace.

The I Ching Divination

Candice had agreed to a meeting with Brian, Teresa and me to talk about the divination she had made. I had imagined a mature, middle-aged lady scholar well versed in all the Chinese classics from ancient times. When we picked her up I was surprised to see that she looked and spoke like a youngster from the neighborhood, slim and athletic, wearing shorts and carrying a big bag.

In the car, Candice and Brian shared how they had met 20 years earlier. Although still in high school, Candice was already very knowledgeable about ancient Chinese texts. One day Brian had arranged to meet someone who had a query about one of his books. Expecting to meet a mature reader, he was surprised when Candice appeared in her school uniform. Later he went on to hire her as his research assistant. Candice recalled that she and other senior scholars had spent many years having fun and leisurely discussions with Brian on the I Ching and other cultural classics.

When we arrived at my place, Candice took a few books from her bag and was ready to talk about the hexagrams of the divination for my situation. My hexagrams were Gradual Progress (53) and Union (8). The former was primary, the latter was procedural (how things evolve towards the end).

The hexagram of Gradual Progress is made up of the image of a tree on a mountain that develops slowly according to the law of its being, and consequently stands firmly rooted. This gives the idea of a development that proceeds gradually, step by step. Candice explained that, in my case, it would be slow. Lawyers and other parties would probably come and visit me, but it would be after a long wait. The pronouncement was in general good, but with a bit of hustle. If I stood firm, things would be fine. She pointed out that there were paragraphs in the scripts (where ancient scholars elaborated on the graphic hexagrams) that were relevant.

Here I quote the translation of the I Ching by Richard Wilhelm, a German sinologist and missionary who lived in China for 25 years and was well versed in the Chinese Classics. He began the translation in 1913 and finished it in 1921. Here is his translation of the first part for H53:

The maiden is given in marriage.
Good fortune.
Perseverance furthers.

This was why Candice had asked Brian whether I was preparing for the wedding of my daughter. I told Candice that my daughter was not getting married, but that a small miracle had happened just two months ago when her menstruation had returned after seven years. I didn't know whether it was relevant here. Candice exclaimed with wide opened eyes, "Oh, that is exactly what the script has said. Your lost daughter is back." In Chinese, there are only six characters in the first sentence of the script: gradual, daughter, back, luck, facilitate stability (漸,女歸吉,利貞。).

In traditional Chinese society, a woman's true home is the one she lives in with her husband. Thus, getting married is described as going back home. Literally, the Chinese characters are simply Daughter / BACK, meaning daughter is back. But the semantically agreed cultural meaning is *getting married*. Now, in my case, it reverts to the literal meaning. And in fact, Constance has been recovering. She is less dependent, and for the first time in seven years she is able to take care of household chores and groceries. I am less worried now about not being able to take care of her if anything happens to me. Thus, intuitively, I thought the script was quite precise in describing my newly emerging domestic situation: the return of my daughter was facilitating stability.

Candice explained that H53 was about gradual progression. Here was the first stage:

The wild goose gradually draws near the plateau.

The man goes forth and does not return.

The woman carries a child but does not bring it forth.

Misfortune.

It furthers one to fight off robbers.

According to Richard Wilhelm's translation, the interpretation is as follows:

"The high plateau is dry and unsuitable for the wild goose. If it goes there, it has lost its way and gone too far. This is contrary to the law of development. It is the same in human life. If we do not let things develop quietly but plunge of our own choice too rashly into a struggle, misfortune results. A man jeopardizes his own life, and his family perishes thereby. However, this is not all necessary; it is only the result of transgressing the law of natural development. If one does not willfully provoke a conflict but confines himself to vigorously maintaining his own position and to warding off unjustified attacks, all goes well."

When Candice made the divination I was still planning to leave the city and test the waters. I told Candice that the script made perfect sense to me. Leaving was risky in this sensitive period. The reference to a pregnant woman resonated in me since the travel plan, with all its minute details, was like a baby about to be born. The plane tickets had been issued and daily accommodation for two months had been confirmed. It was almost the literal meaning of the verses: "The man goes forth and does not return. The woman carries a child but does not bring it forth." Candice stressed, "The advice is clear, please stay put. You'd better cancel the trip." I told her I already had.

The final stage is written in the following verses:

The wild goose gradually draws near the cloud heights.

Its feathers can be used for the sacred dance.

Good fortune.

Feathers are used for ritualistic decoration. Candice's interpretation was that the stakeholders who pressed charges would pluck a feather from me and use my case as a ritual or a formality, but they would not inflict substantial harm on me. Candice remarked: "It's a feather they pluck, not your wings or heart. It is not fatal."

I had a very different interpretation. I didn't know whether it was wishful thinking motivated by my desire to be off the hook or whether it was a reflection of the spiritual journey I had just begun, but my hunch was that the feathers were the lessons I had learned so far and would be learning throughout the process. And these precious feathers – a divine gift given to me – would be used for "the sacred dance" that all pilgrims sharing the lessons learned on their respective spiritual paths join. Time would tell which interpretation would unfold.

Then the secondary and procedural H8: Holding together, which is supposed to be a projection of the final stage of the development.

Holding together brings good fortune.

Inquire of the oracle once again

Whether you possess sublimity, constancy, and perseverance;

Then there is no blame.
Those who are uncertain gradually join.
Whoever comes too late
Meets with misfortune.

Candice explained that this was just to remind me to stay with the group (holding together) and lie low, don't fall behind alone. The I Ching is the Book of Changes, and as time passes zillions of factors are in flux, situations are changing, and people will change paths. Candice said, "When this final stage approaches, we will see how it goes."

Reading this script, the Chinese character Yuen stood out to me. Richard Wilhelm translated it as sublimity. I remembered Brian, a devoted Buddhist, talking about an inner state of being where one was back to "square one", or back to Yuen. This Chinese character refers to the source, the original and the One. And this reminded me of the experience I had had just yesterday beside the camphor tree. I had found a timeless state of being, of sublimity. I remembered the word Yuen had appeared in my mind at that moment of grace. It made a well-fit handle of the experience. It had only been the day before, and that indescribable experience was still very fresh in me. I intuitively connected with this Hexagram of union, but I was not sure of the practical implications. I guessed it might be a reminder for me to hold on to "sublimity, constancy and perseverance" till the end, "then there is no blame".

The Unfolding Dream

On the Wednesday I went hiking with the group of retirees as usual. I had been doing this weekly activity for quite some time. Resuming after three months of Covid partial lockdown, some of us, including me, found the steep climb quite difficult. Besides the physical demands, I had considerable disquiet about my case, which shortened my breath and unsettled my heart. The very thought of the danger was like a sword hanging over my head. I needed to do more than mindful walking to ease myself.

Anxiety is like a seed, says Zen master Thich Nhat Hanh. When triggered, it becomes a mental formation which gets bigger and bigger in our consciousness. Suppressing it does no good. It will simply break out again with stronger force. Nature has the capacity to take in negativity and breathe life into us. I had read quite a lot of the Zen master's teaching on mental formation, but this was the first time I had seriously put the teachings into practice. Slow burning anxiety came back again and again. I had to keep on taking care of these not so strong but persistent emotions. With some practice, it worked, and more so when I was accustomed to mindful breathing along the way.

I have been a newspaper columnist for more than 30 years; however, I never mastered the skill of typing in Chinese. I have always submitted handwritten texts. This is old school. Now all young columnists submit electronically. A few years back I started to write more about emotional wellbeing, and this was well received by readers, much more than any of my other writings. Then came the prolonged pandemic. I had a strong sense of a divine calling to write for broken hearts and wounded souls. I even changed my mode of writing – I stopped planning and waited for contents to unfold. I was a messenger, relaying a message given to me. Then when I became enmeshed in this business my friends advised me not to write. So, I stopped. But what about my calling? Was it real? Or was it just my egoic yearning to do some good for my beloved city?

Strolling through the woodland I attended to my breathing and bodily sensations, which felt like following hidden trails. Something was there, yet unclear. Dreamy images they were, whispering from the inside of me. I was walking, but it seemed like I was dreaming.

Gradually, that something became clear. Graphic images came to my mind, almost like a vision. I had the felt sense of typing in English about my spiritual journey – not my usual routine of handwriting my essays in Chinese. It was a vivid sensation of typing in solitude. It felt right. And I wondered, was this a new calling?

I kept on climbing the slope. Whenever I came upon open space, I grounded myself and surrendered to the big blue sky and the vast wilderness. The sensation of typing, the sound of the keyboard, the pondering and revising were vividly *there*.

It came to me that toying with an English manuscript had been in a dream I had had two months ago, the contents of which had faded into a black hole. I could remember nothing except for the sensation of flipping through the English script. What was that dream about? With some effort, I remembered.

In the dream, something unusual had happened. City traffic had stopped and the highways were empty. Passengers were queuing up at bus stops but no bus was coming. There was a tense mood in the air. The sky was dark with apocalyptic rain clouds engulfing streets and buildings. It was a lock down.

In the dream, I was invited by a famous director to revise a movie script. I was full of confidence that I could finish it by the next day. At a sidewalk café I was totally immersed in dealing with the script, which was in English. I was revising it with the paper facing down, reading the sentences from the back of a piece of semi-luminous paper; the sentences thus appeared as a mirror image with words spelled backward, in reverse.

I didn't understand what the dream was about at that time. The director is famous for making movies on local Hakka culture. All his scripts are in Chinese. How come he asked me to work on his English movie script in the dream? But now, two months later, hiking on the trail with the new idea of writing of my spiritual journey in English, the dream unveiled itself.

I had a feeling that I had to write in English about what was unfolding in my life, with names changed like a true fable in an alien city.

I had this movie script dream two months ago. Was it precognition? Or had it transformed to become a vision now? I didn't have a clue to its meaning before, but now it felt right. Whether it was a precognition or a vision didn't matter; it was an invitation for me to document my spiritual journey, and I was more than willing to accept the challenge.

Something Beyond Words

At the time of this realization, I had been reading Eckhart Tolle's *The Power of Now* and found extraordinary affirmation there. Had I started reading earlier I would have stopped right after the introduction because the description of his spiritual awakening would have been too outlandish to me. His biographical sketch in the introduction is interesting, but the chapters that follow would have sounded abstract and remote to me. I was skeptical when Clara guided us to connect with trees. When she mentioned cosmic energy, the spiritual self, the energy from the soil and such, I didn't know what she was referring to. I tried to comprehend the meaning or the "entity" that the words signified, but I could find nothing behind the words no matter how hard I tried to envision them.

But after my experience in front of the big camphor tree, and my subsequent, less strong but still quite substantial, experience of the spiritual self, Tolle's writings make a lot of sense now. He says that we are in the spiritual dimension when we are not thinking, when we are free from the mind, when we can observe our ego and be the witness to our emotions from a spacious vantage point which is beyond time. He says that we will sense the oneness with nature and that we are a part of the whole.

During those brief moments I spent beside the camphor tree I felt all of the above.

Tolle describes these experiences in words. Of course, spiritual experiences are beyond words. I have only had a glimpse. I don't have words to describe my awakening, I am just there, being. After reading Tolle's book three things are clear:

First, there is an awareness beyond my active mind, my psyche, and my physical body. In that state I can be a witness to my egoic activities, observing my thoughts and my emotions.

Second, there is energy in the air and under the soil. It flows through me. It is *Chi* in the Taoist tradition. It is the movement of energy from the source, the un-manifest – which I didn't know before. Now I am familiar with the sensation of flowing energies. When I am attentive, it is inside and beyond me.

Third, the inner body. In the past few years I have learned a lot about the functioning of the mind and the body. Modern life favors the analytic power of the left brain while the intuitive capacity of the right brain has been largely suppressed. The practice of Eugene Gendlin's Focusing is very much a return to the felt sense and the wisdom of the body. Gendlin's body, in the terminology of neuroscience, is the summation of the sensory receptors, somatic reflexivity, and the neuro-circuitry coordinated by some unique features of the right brain. The return to the wisdom of the body echoes Eckhart Tolle's idea of the inner body where the spiritual self resides.

Words are pointers, describing the state of being in vague suggestions. In fact, I didn't recognize my experience as an awakening when it happened. It took me quite a while to venture to describe the camphor tree moment as an "awakening," for it is too big a word for me. After some research and reading I found that a lot of people have had similar experiences. It is not as exotic as I had thought.

On a personal level, it has a qualitative difference from other spiritual experiences I had before. As a 21-year-old freshman in a theological seminary, I walked back and forth on the rooftop terrace of the students' dormitory one night. The seminary was on a remote island far away from the glaring city lights. Under the starry sky I was in meditation as I walked. At that time, I had not yet heard of the term mindful walking, but I guess I did exactly that. The stars were bright and seemed near, as if I could reach out to them. I made a vow to dedicate myself to sharing whatever gift life would give me. I had no idea what that gift might be, but I had made up my young mind to this life-time goal. Suddenly my mind was as clear as the starry sky. I was like a fish jumping out of the water and seeing the amazing galaxy for the first time. My normal life was underwater, so to speak, and I wasn't aware of the water in which I swam. At that moment, out of the water, all my bodily sensations were sharpened – the air was clean, the breeze caring, horizon broadened, eyes wide open. It was calm and quiet. Put beside the camphor tree moment, the calmness is the same but at the seminary I didn't sense the presence of a spiritual self and the distancing of the ego. At that blissful moment my young mind was filled with a grand life mission of doing something meaningful for the world.

This time the awakening is different. There is a self, calm and at ease, but the boundary between the self and the rest of the world is not that clear. It is not self vs other, but self and the world connected, the inter-being of men and nature, as Thich Nhat Hanh once said. The awareness of presence is not filled up with thoughts and plans. There is no time, and the mind is not thinking. Within the calmness of the spiritual self, ego is still there, but it is no longer what one is anchored to in life.

Chapter 5

The In-between Space Beyond Social Science

Remain in the Vine

"Remain in me, as I also remain in you. No branch can bear fruit by itself; it must remain in the vine. Neither can you bear fruit unless you remain in me." (Gospel of John 15:4)

Most of us have heard stories of friends turning to Jesus or Buddha when they have a near-death accident or illness, or an encounter with extreme undercurrents in life. Some switch to a healthy diet or even vow to turn vegan when diagnosed with cancer. But quite often, once the threat has gone, a switch back to the banality of old habits happens. Some become devoted Christians or Buddhists for good, some return to their secular life when adversity is no more. So, I wonder: are their spiritual experiences merely a psychological escape? Isn't it the case that once the danger has gone, the "awakening" no longer serves its soothing purpose? Put another way, is it difficult, in Jesus's parable, for the branches to remain in the vine? Is the spiritual bonding here to stay or is it psychological, compensatory and thus temporary?

I was a devoted Christian when I was young, and I knew that verse from the *Gospel of John* by heart. Growing up in church had been a bittersweet experience. There were peaceful and joyous moments, but a lot of guilt, shame and self-criticism too. It was very difficult for me to "remain in the vine". I graduated from a theological seminary, and now, after almost 40 years, I still keep up with some of my good friends from my class, most of whom are pastors in churches and professors in seminaries in K-Town and abroad. Yes, they had the experience of being summoned by God to their vocation but after graduation a few, like me, left the Church. As far as I know, many of my former classmates have been faithful, doing good in their churches and in society at large. But most of them are no longer as strict in the religious sense as before. As we have grown older, my friends have become more relaxed and they've told me interesting stories from their Christian circles. It is quite funny to hear that some of the most influential pastors (nicknamed "Big Logs," for *pastor* in Chinese begins with the homophone "wood") have big egos, and yell at their deacons for not giving them the most prominent seat at big ceremonies. Demanding respect is only the most harmless thing those Big Logs would do. The craziest thing I heard was that the disgraced head of a seminary ruined his successor's inauguration ceremony by starting a rumor of a bomb scare at the site of the ceremony. The police came, the ceremony was stopped, the congregation was dispersed.

These few leaders with big egos, are they still servants of God? Are they remaining in the vine? If you think these stories of the Big Logs are too remote from your own experience, let me put it this way: If we have an awakening or an inspiration to live differently, would it be a momentary thing? Would it be just a spark of zeal which quickly burns out?

When I was still a practicing Christian I had quite a few spiritual experiences of sincere repentance, deep gratitude, of recognizing God's calling me to be a pastor, of guidance at the crossroads of my life, etc. But remaining in the vine was hard for me. These epiphanies, no matter how fervently I felt at that moment, turned into obstacles instead, for they seemed to be so transitory and volatile. Life is difficult. Tranquility is just an occasional relief in rough seas. For many years, I let my Christian faith lie dormant, just leaving it there – not to the extent of renunciation, but seeing it as irrelevant, restrictive and even misleading. I am still open to the spiritual, but I don't think spirituality can be contained under any specific religious institution.

After my awakening, something inside me is here to stay. A spiritual self it is – calm, connected with the One, beyond time, accessible only a breath away, and abiding in me all the time. I know that state of being and I can discern that presence much more easily than before. Of course, sometimes there is anxiety when thoughts of adversity rush into my mind, when it rains hard for days as though sadness is trailing through the sky, when friends leave for good and things fall apart. Nostalgia is painful and hurts. It takes some practice to look into these feelings deeply without the urge to discipline or reject them; to just take a few breaths and to acknowledge that my spiritual self is here, inside of me, staying apart from the rise and fall of emotions.

The Inner Critic

After dinner, I took a walk with Constance. Again, her inner critic had been very active, accusing her of not reading enough and being stupid and lazy. This round of trivial but heated accusation was triggered by a trifling exchange between Constance and her friend and colleague Ann, who asked Constance's opinion on whether to buy a new book. Constance's inner critic's reaction was immediate, reminding Constance herself that there was a pile of books she had bought, still on the shelf unread. This inner critic has been here for a very long time. Earlier on it would blend in amongst other voices. Now that Constance's psychological condition is much better, she can locate its distinctive voice.

We hadn't done an Internal Family System (IFS) exercise for quite a while and I had a hunch we could do it at the waterfront. IFS is a therapy originated by psychotherapist Richard Schwartz, who expanded his expertise in family therapy into an operational model of IFS in the 1980s. After decades of accumulation, IFS is no longer a fringe alternative but a respectable therapeutic approach to a variety of emotional and personality issues.

Schwartz acknowledges that we have different subpersonalities (*parts*) within us. Some carry and hide away wounds and traumas (*exiles*), some defend and motivate us (*protectors*), some use extreme measures to stop our pain and suffering (*firefighters*). The aim of this approach is to help us identify and befriend these parts so that they won't behave in an unhelpful way.

I have taken two IFS courses, the elementary and the advanced, and find the techniques safe and user-friendly. The inner critic is a common *protector* that motivates us to excel, but it often does this by invoking shame and guilt. As Constance's inner critic was agitated, I sensed that it was a good time to let "him" talk. We did a brief grounding exercise and I invited the critic to talk directly to me. At once Constance spoke in the harsh tone of this inner critic, complaining with a sharp tongue. Behind the fury, I sensed disappointment, sadness, and frustration.

Following some basic IFS techniques, I tried to relate with the inner critic, not by combating his anger but with curiosity and empathy. As Schwartz stresses all *parts* are welcome. They are here for a reason, they would like to serve, yet more often than not they are locked inside an outdated crisis, and stubbornly use the same defensive mechanism to respond to every new situation.

Constance's inner critic has been around for many years, criticizing her for not performing up to standard, for being unable to honor her promises, and for failing to maintain her self-perceived identity as a competent learner. I asked the inner critic when he had first come into Constance's life. I had imagined he was "born" as a *protector* at the time of her major trauma in high school, but to my surprise the critic confessed that he had come along much earlier, when she was still a young child.

Constance had had vivid violent images flashing in her head from as early as she could remember. Those images were overwhelming, such as pushing other kids onto the railway, and cutting family members with a knife. There was also a strong disciplinary voice prohibiting her from doing harm to others. That is to say, from a very young age she had felt guilty about her involuntary impulses to hurt people close to her. Her inner critic had already been activated long before the trauma she experienced in high school. Knowing this piece of information about the *protector* was useful. It would help Constance to "un-blend", an IFS saying for maintaining a distance between the self and this dominating subpersonality.

I have read Thich Nhat Han's teaching on inter-being – that our existences are connected with others of our time and even with the heritage of our ancestors. Constance told me she had had those violent images since her childhood. We didn't know why, and still don't. A few years ago an assessment was made when Constance started seeing her psychiatrist. At that time those violent images had been less frequent and so didn't appear to be a concern. But that evening, conversing with her inner critic, I was curious about where those violent images had come from. When they began she was just a child not yet exposed to violent movies or television. What was the source of these images?

This IFS dialogue with Constance acting the role of the critic may have triggered a piece of forgotten memory for her. As we walked along the sidewalk by the sea, she suddenly remembered that in First Grade, when she was six, her teacher talked about a piece of news in class: a bus had mounted the sidewalk and a pedestrian had been knocked over and was crushed under the wheel. Constance told me that as she listened to her teacher, she was literally there, standing in front of the body, seeing the pool of blood. She had that image in her head, a vivid sense and sight. She was scared.

The following week in her composition class she wrote a first-person account of the dying man in vivid terms. Her shocked teacher asked what had happened to her. But, in fact, it was only that she had heard the news and was able to visualize the scene and vicariously experience the trauma from a first-person perspective. I wonder, is Constance's life bundled with others? Are there patterns of behavior, thoughts and memories "precipitated" into her life from beyond? Can there be elements passed on to Constance, not through genes or her upbringing, but via channels unknown to us?

Synchronicity, an Ethnographic Reflection

As a social scientist, synchronistic experiences, which generate meanings in coincidences, have been difficult for me to comprehend. Social research is a rigorous effort to do the opposite, to find meanings in routines and behaviors which co-exist not by chance but by regularity. Social reality is in constant flux. In any given situation there are more contributing factors than a researcher can handle. The best s/he can do is to find out whether two occurrences have a high or low statistical correlation.

However, as situations change with time and space so does correlation. Human beings are reflexive, they learn and adapt, making it even more difficult to find stable behavioral patterns. Nevertheless, social researchers try very hard to work against this seeming randomness and find correlational patterns that are relatively stable. One end of the spectrum is causal relationship: the other end, mere coincidence. Social scientists try to point towards causality, but the best they can attain is high statistical probabilities.

Synchronicity, however, is non-causal. Physical and mental happenings co-exist in parallel. A thought, an image in a dream, or a song overheard from next door, these intangible symbols manifest themselves in the actual world all the time. They seem to be random, mere coincidences, but sometimes the person involved has a sudden insight so real and timely that others wouldn't be able to understand.

This is in big contrast to what the social scientists have in mind. The logic is different. So is the whole conception of the life world we are in. In a synchronistic world, unrelated things and people are related in a network of meaning unexplainable to modern man. Long before modernity, men and women were more receptive to the reciprocal exchange between the psyche and the world. Intuition, myth, connectivity, embodiment, wholeness, heritage, etc. are all conducive to synchronicities. Random events like a thunderstorm, a dream, or a butterfly resting on the floor, when they manifest at a moment are meaningful to the beholder and may be seen as a profound message by a mystic, though the man on the street will write them off as random occurrences.

Last November several unrelated incidents in my family unfolded with great intensity in a single week. Despite my deep-seated conviction about researchable regularities, I was thrown into a world of synchronicity, of utterly unrelated happenings, yet which were deeply meaningful to me to the extent that I had to change lanes immediately, to ponder the priorities of my pursuit, which in turn changed the path of my life.

These synchronicities are covered in the previous chapters, here I just briefly recap:

- My dear cat's retina came off and she went blind the day the investigators came, dying three days later on the evening the sky turned a stunning purplish red.

- Constance photographed that sky, as did many others that evening. The picture appeared accompanying the last essay of my column which I had written for 22 years. Sent as a thank you to the editor, she mistook my intention and printed the photo with my farewell essay.
- Before cremation, when I saw my cat in her casket, I came to the realization that, with her eyes closed and her round face turned diamond-shaped due to dehydration, she looked like a lamb, just like the sacrificial lamb I dreamed of six months ago. In the dream the lamb was a peace offering – for my family or for the city I was not sure.
- In November last year Candice made a divination for Brian with the message for both of us to lay low, and we did.
- In April this year, right after the senior executives of the parent company were formally accused of a crime, Candice made divinations for each of us. Oddly, even though we were in the same situation, my reading was different from Brian's. It was spot on about my daughter's condition and about my plan to leave the city.
- All these overlapped with a weeklong self-care program that I took, where Clara talked about trees as welcoming and compassionate beings and channels of energy.
- My camphor tree moment of awakening came at the end of that chaotic week in April, which marked a new beginning in my spiritual journey.

How could I make sense of the synchronistic experiences listed above? From a materialist point of view these are all unrelated coincidences. One might say I read the cat into my dream with my strong intent to connect. My cat and the sacrificial lamb were just two separate images. So was the gorgeous sunset. However, except for small incidents like these two, which I could explain as the wish fulfillment of my own intentionality, most of the occurrences colliding into each other were improbable.

For instance, the I Ching Hexagram is difficult to explain. Candice threw the coins by pure chance to get the 53/8 Hexagram. The script matched the immediate events in my family. The news of senior staff being charged and my attending the self-care course were totally unrelated, but happened in parallel before my Zoom class. The exercises on the course were preparing me to deal with the intense anxiety I faced. My psychological and spiritual states have been notably altered by these synchronicities, whose profound meanings are solid and of great significance to my life.

When I was in academia, teaching at the university, one of my areas of expertise was ethnography, a method adopted by anthropologists to understand a culture, community or tribe by staying among them for long enough to be able to share and make sense of their daily exchanges. While quantitative researchers use surveys, statistical tools and controllable experiments, ethnographers follow the qualitative logic of using the researchers' own subjectivity to measure against the informants they are researching. That is to say, when the ethnographers get to know the informants, and find out that their own cognitive and emotive schemes don't explain or fit in with their new experiences in the field, they have to adjust themselves and see the world from the perspective of the informants. That is why the ethnographer welcomes conflicts and discrepancies, for these dissonances are the sources of new knowledge and the raw materials for a *thick* description of new ethnographic understanding.

In my previous projects, my informants were members of underground bands, migrant workers and cultural brokers. This time the informant is my good self. The ethnographic lens is turned onto my own spiritual experiences. I would like to follow this ethnographic logic to make sense of synchronicity, making some initial inferences as far as my experiences will allow.

Meaningful coincidences are seen by those with intuitive openness. Intuition is not mysterious; our right brain, the neuro-circuitry and the receptors all over our body are capable of knowing beyond words. Candice told me that the most important thing about I Ching divination is that she has to empty herself and be pure at heart when she throws the three coins or counts through the forty-nine yarrow stalks. In that way there is a channel between the observer and the immediate world, not blocked by preconceptions, knowledge, and convictions.

I have practiced Eugene Gendlin's meditative Focusing, which is a way to get in touch with the felt sense of the body and derive meaning from the somatic self instead of the rational mind. Often I can find unexpected connections between the psyche and the physical world. From my own experiences, intuition is the direct and immediate awareness of meaningful links between unrelated images or events, and that, I guess, is the basis of synchronicity.

Behind chance and randomness, synchronicity has a connectivity of its own. The I Ching is built on this randomness of the moment and maps out the connectivity of various probable events in 64 hexagrams. In his introduction to Richard Wilhelm's translation, Carl Jung wrote: "The ancient Chinese mind contemplates the cosmos in a way comparable to that of the modern physicist, who cannot deny that his model of the world is a decidedly psychophysical structure. The microphysical event includes the observer just as much as the reality underlying the I Ching comprises subjective, i.e., psychic conditions in the totality of the momentary situation. Just as causality describes the sequence of events, so synchronicity to the Chinese mind deals with the coincidence of events." When a particular hexagram is cast, it becomes the exponent of the moment, somewhat like an index that you can connect to the web of things.

When I opened the door to the investigators my cat was lying on the dining table facing the door. She stared at them and didn't move. On a thousand occasions, whenever friends or strangers knocked on the door, my cat would dash away to her hiding place in a second. At that moment she didn't act in her usual way and stayed on the table motionless. Then she went blind. The probable explanation was that she was in great fear, her blood pressure shot up and her retina fell off. But her death was linked with a network of meaningful coincidences listed above.

In our everyday reality these incidents are random, without any causal relation. In the world of synchronicity, the random moment of my cat meeting the eyes of the investigators began a chain reaction interconnected with a lot of things of grave meaning to our family.

Here is a quote from Mark Nepo, a poet and author of the bestseller *The Book of Awakening,* which tells us of the life and energy of a random moment in poetic fullness.

"Random is the instant a horse at full speed has all four hooves off the ground."

"So, what might we learn from the horse at random? Consider how all its energy and desire mounts for the moment it inhabits itself fully, and in that moment, it flies. Only to touch down again. And to fly again. And touch down again. For us, the moment at random is the moment of holding nothing back, of giving our all to whatever situation is before us. In that charged moment, we come as close to flying as human beings can – we soar briefly with a passion for life that brings everything within us to meet our daily world."

The In-between Space

In her insightful book, *The Extended Mind,* acclaimed science writer Annie Murphy Paul argues that we have been using our head too much, and that it is much more fruitful if we think outside the brain. What she means is engaging "entities" outside our heads – the spaces we are in, the feelings and movements of our bodies, the hearts, and minds of other people around us.

"By reaching beyond the brain to recruit these 'extra-neural' resources, we are able to focus more intently, comprehend more deeply, and create more imaginatively – to entertain ideas that would be literally unthinkable by the brain alone."

Her thesis is that we can think *with* and *through* our bodies, our spaces, and our relationships. Her writings ring a bell in me. That is what goes on within me during my practices of Focusing, meditating, and working on dreams. In my experience, it is not just thinking outside my brain; I have also been extending my awareness and sensibility into the spaces within and outside of me.

For some time I have had more experiences of this in-between space. It is a space between my awareness and my physical body, between my inner self and the life world I am in. I guess this space can be felt with the naivety and instinct of a baby, but as we have been exhorted to use our heads more and more, we have hampered our multi-faceted sense-perception from a young age.

This in-between space was unfamiliar to me before, apart from some occasions which I would categorize as paranormal and inexplicable. For instance, I had an out of body experience when I was in my mid-thirties. I was skinny and always felt cold. I wore a jacket even in the heat of summer. Movie producer JP, a good friend, knew of a talented healer living on the outskirts of K-Town, who claimed that "Tian" (heaven or gods) gave him healing powers and he pledged to treat people for free. At that time, I was adventurous about these types of things.

I found myself in a small apartment in a village with JP and Teresa by my side. The healer started my session by offering incense and praying to his gods. When he pressed his fingers on the soles of my feet, it was just like a nail piercing my skin. I literally dropped flat on the sofa and fainted. It was instant and dramatic. My consciousness went out of my body. I was up in the air, peaceful and weightless, without mass.

In no time, I floated through the wall of the second floor and was outside the building, a dozen meters above ground, looking down at the street below. It was a narrow alley with small shops in gloomy light. There were people talking, but I felt quiet and all alone. I glided slowly forward until I heard JP yelling, "Manny! Come back!" He called my full name in Hakka Chinese. I heard him and was back on the sofa instantly, in shock. The first sentence out of my mouth was, "Where am I?" Firmly holding my hands was JP, eyes wide open. Teresa was by my side too. According to her account, my face turned pale and my lips were purple when I was "unconscious".

JP, a practicing Buddhist, said he had had an impulse to call me back at that moment. As we left, he told me that the healer had whispered to him that something was inside me. Three of them, apparently. They were not hostile, but just taking shelter there, and now, "They are gone, you are cleansed."

As we walked along the alley, I was interested to notice that I had been here a short while ago, only the view had been from a dozen meters above. We had reached the healer from the other side of the alley – this part should have been new to us, but I found the shops were the ones I had seen some moments earlier.

This out-of-body experience never happened again. At the time I didn't take it seriously. I didn't buy into the healer's explanation that three entities had been expelled from me, but my physiological changes after this out-of-body experience were significant: I gained weight, and my feet and hands are generally much warmer than before.

After my sublime moment before the camphor tree, I am much more aware of my daughter's sensitivity to the spiritual realms and of my own experiences with the in-between space that is beyond the materiality of things.

First and foremost, there is a space between my inner self and my ego, the conscious "me" I have known for years. Before, there was no such space. My ego was there at the seat of awareness. Now there is an inner self, a sublime state similar to my out-of-body experience and to that of my awakening before the giant tree. I am calm and at ease, having a vantage point from which to witness the activities of the ego.

Second, there is a space that I can sense between my loved ones – my wife and especially my daughter, who share an intuitive sensitivity towards the parapsychological – and I. For the past seven years I have talked with my daughter about her disorder, using various therapeutic methods. I can sense her moods and thoughts without being physically next to her. Sometimes we picture the same thing in our mind without verbal communication. While using IFS therapy, when several *protectors* inside her are active, very different vibes can be in the air, emitted from each of them simultaneously. Experienced IFS therapists do share this kind of non-verbal sensitivity.

Third, in a meditative state, the feeling of oneness is quite common. I am connected to all living beings like birds, trees, friends, and others, as a peaceful whole. Yet I am not completely merged into something else; I am still here, and it is spacious, and we are one. I am part of nature, not an observer or visitor.

Fourth, when I am experiencing synchronicities, especially those with precognitive elements, there is a sense of articulation between different temporal and spatial planes. I have a dream at point (a), then something totally unrelated happens at point (b), then yet another thing unfolds at point (c). The sequential timing of these three is linear, but (a) plus (b) plus (c) start to make sense, as if they make up a single event, free from the limiting effect of time.

The peace offering dream was in an in-between space articulating the image of a sacrificial lamb and my cat at her funeral. My experience with the I Ching divination exhibited a much more elaborate web in an in-between space consisting of Candice, the threat I was facing, my daughter's rejuvenation, my aborted travel plan, and a big leap in my spiritual journey, threaded together by the hexagrams written in ancient times.

Looking back, I was taking some baby steps in my spiritual journey, stretching my sensibility into the edge of my awareness. By practicing mindful attention to these in-between spaces, I have opened up my rather restrictive mind-set as a social science scholar, and got a taste of synchronicities and providence, not in big metaphysical claims, but with tangible ethnographic heuristics.

身病心不病

Chapter 6

The Limpid Light of the Plum Village Dream

The Plum Village Dream

I woke in the early hours with the dream still vivid. I sensed its strangeness and relevance to me and the city, so I wrote it down before going back to sleep.

The dream has two discrete scenes.

Scene 1: I am inside a brightly lit hall at Plum Village with a large group of people I don't know. The wall is painted white with vertical stripes in light yellow. We are divided into small groups for discussion and activities. I am assigned to a group in which a young monk talks about how peace could be spread around the world to reduce violence. The monk says we can do it by practicing mindfulness, with Plum Village as a starting point.

I think the monk is too naïve. Mindfulness won't be a cure for the problems of the world. But then I have a strange realization in the dream: despite the monk's idealism, he is correct. I speak up loudly about my insight to everyone in the hall. I proclaim in a very loud voice, "He is correct, despite his idealism..." I catch the attention of the whole crowd in the hall. Then I think I just spoke too much and too loudly. I shut up and sit in silence.

Scene 2: There is a disturbing noise outside. Something bad must have happened. Everyone in the hall is holding their breath. A tall guy with very big ears rushes in. Someone escorts him to a safe place next to the hall. We see there is blood all over his head, especially his ears. A guy with a flashlight is asking Frank (my former colleague, a well-known professor) to clear the way. Frank is sitting on a chair leaning against the wall. It is urgent, but he doesn't get it, sitting there dumbfounded, so I pull his chair together with him, away from the wall so that he won't block the passageway. The wall is in fact a partition with large rectangular openings to let the sunlight shine in.

The guy uses the flashlight to guide and encourage a band of frightened dogs from the outside to come into the hall through those openings. Dozens of dogs hop in, and the last two are lambs. One by one, they take refuge inside, disoriented and fearful.

In the dream, I don't know how I knew what the animals had gone through. I just knew. People who live nearby are hostile to the monks and nuns. Whenever the monastery holds a retreat like this one, the citizens of the city organize big wildfire feasts, killing and roasting dogs and lambs on open ground. They want to undo the redemptive activities undertaken inside Plum Village. The animals are rescued from one of these feasts by friends from the village. I guess the guy covered with blood was the rescuer.

Towards the end of the dream, I see a guy calming one of the two trembling lambs by covering it with a blanket. The other lamb is right in front of me, resting on a table, trembling. It is about to die. Its wool is gray in color, covered with dust. I am pleased to see so many lovely animals being saved, and I have a lot of compassion towards this dying lamb. I make a vow to respect living beings with care and love, just as the monks and nuns do.

Then I wake up.

The dream seemed quite full of latent meanings that I couldn't comprehend by myself, so I invited Cliff, Liz, Peggy and Ed to do some dreamwork with me. They knew about the threat I was facing, and some of my past dreams. With their help, I hoped I could discover more about my Plum Village dream.

The Limpid Light

Cliff and Liz had recently emigrated to Australia. While settling down, they took a break in France to attend the 40th anniversary of the Plum Village Retreat in early June. A decade ago, they had spent a whole year there and Plum Village has been a kind of second home to them. That was why I was eager to have them hear this dream. We all met via Zoom and I shared my dream without adding any context. I just wanted them to respond to the dream itself.

Listening to my dream, Cliff commented that it was as if I were at Plum Village. "No," he corrected himself, "It is not *as if*. You actually *are there*. That is how I feel."

Liz, bursting with excitement, asked if I had received the letter she'd sent me from Plum Village. I said that I hadn't. I hadn't opened the mailbox for a few weeks. She told me that they had sent me a postcard saying: '*We brought you to the retreat*.' I smiled and thanked her. "I guess the card is sitting there now, waiting for me to collect it."

I had in my mind an amusing but perplexing feeling of synchronicity. In the dream, I was in France, while physically I was in K-Town with the French postcard in my mailbox for weeks. Plum Village was far away – Plum Village was near at hand. Somehow, the monastery is a physical place as well as a spiritual space, through which like-minded practitioners can connect with each other beyond time and space. It seemed that the words Liz and Cliff had written had actually taken me there in my dream.

Cliff was touched by the dying lamb, which reminded him of his stay at Plum Village ten years ago. A heavy burden on his shoulders at that time had made him want to leave his tiresome life in K-Town for a year. Once, while resting on the floor of the empty temple at midnight, he had thought it would be a blessing if he could die peacefully inside the village.

He imagined being the dying lamb and seeing the world through its eyes: the lamb's short life had accomplished nothing of huge significance. It had narrowly escaped being killed in the BBQ rally, and now its life would come to an end inside this peaceful sanctuary. "What a blessing." Cliff spoke as if he was witnessing the death of this imaginary lamb.

I hadn't thought of that, but Cliff's feeling resonated deeply inside me. In the dream, I wasn't sad. I had no fear, I had a lot of compassion, but I just couldn't put my feelings into words. Cliff articulated what was inside me and helped bring up the emotion lucidly.

Yes, I told myself, it was worthwhile for the lamb to be in this world. There is no need to strive for big achievements in secular eyes. Completing the journey was already a big accomplishment, and having a humble but noble end in the caring hands of the monks and nuns was a real blessing.

I recalled that, before Cliff left K-Town for Australia last November, we had a Focusing session during which I said a poignant prayer, speaking as if I were the sacrificial lamb in my dream. That was in the hectic week when I first learned of the grave legal threat I was mixed up in. I felt that solemn moment of dying decently, a life accomplished, on a sacred altar. At a critical juncture of our life journey, there was a moment when we each were so very close to the felt sense of sacrificial dying. Tears were in my eyes. Cliff's too.

We had all been practicing Eugene Gendlin's Focusing method, which is the reason that we came together as a group of brothers and sisters. We are used to paying attention to our felt sense while talking to each other. This is what Cliff does. He listened to my dream while sensing his own somatic reactions. In everyday language, it is similar to "opening our hearts," but in Focusing we are "listening to the wisdom of the body," by attuning to our holistic sensation. Empathic sharing in dreamwork can help the dreamer to go deeper into the implicit realm of the unconscious.

The flashlight caught Cliff's attention. Again, without his empathic listening I would have left out this tiny piece of detail. Cliff said flashlights are commonly used in Plum Village as a simple and crude tool for lighting, and, as in the context of my dream, as a guiding light for disoriented animals. I have never been to Plum Village and had no idea that flashlights were used there. Banal and ordinary as it is, not heroic or dramatic, the monks see this peace-giving and life-saving act as a natural thing that they do. The beauty lies in its simplicity. The flashlight is a mesmerizing image of humanitarian compassion in a humble form.

To my surprise, Liz told us that during the retreat in France a month ago there had been a discussion similar to the one in the first part of my dream. A group of activists from different parts of the world had gathered to discuss what they could offer to their respective societies as spiritual practitioners. Some came from war zones, others from societies with turbulent crises. The Zen teacher's response was that practicing mindfulness was the way. Friends in the group were not satisfied with this answer. The world is riven with complicated financial, racial, and political crises. Mindfulness as a way out seems too simple and naïve. In my dream, that same kind of dissatisfaction was there. It felt surreal to know that Liz had had that emotion in the actual retreat. I had dreamed of something that happened in a faraway place, a meaningful coincidence crosscutting the psychological and the physical. But of course, it is not that unusual for people in a retreat to debate about social engagement.

Liz and Peggy shared the same feeling a few years back, when they had doubts about the great teachings of Thich Nhat Hanh. At times, spiritual practice of any sort seemed futile in the face of brutal social confrontations. What benefit was there in meditation for people afflicted by violence and discrimination? Is mindful practice really a way out of antagonism?

Surely, this is a big social-vs-spiritual debate. To many of us it is not an either/or question. We can be socially engaged and spiritually mindful. But the challenging question is whether spirituality has an effective role to play in large scale crises, such as a crippling pandemic. The idea of Plum-Village-vs-the-rest-of-the-world is too simple a dichotomy. For many, mindfulness is not an effective remedy for dealing with complications and abnormalities across ethnicities, cultures and nations.

As for my dreamwork in that meeting, I didn't want to get into this analytic debate. Dreams operate best in the sublime and liminal realm, not in the analytical. My friends asked me to go back to the part in my dream when I shouted, "Despite the idealism, he is correct!" They wanted to know what I had felt at that moment.

For me, *idealism* is a word that carries some negative connotations. It is raw. It simplifies things. In the dream, was I agreeing with what the Zen master was saying? In academia, in cultural and social studies in particular, idealism is a negative label for over-simplification, similar to the dichotomization of the Western vs the oriental world; the good vs the evil; modernity vs traditionalism; and in this case, the spiritual vs the secular world. If I ever uttered the word idealistic to my postgraduate students it was as a mild criticism for research that I felt was not sophisticated enough. But in my dream, I had a feeling of suchness when I exhorted in a loud voice, "Idealistic, but correct," – that the spiritual practice of peace could cut across atrocities, no matter how complicated the situations might appear. That is to say, in my rational mind, I disagree with the teacher, but my felt sense in the dream was that the teacher is right.

When I told my friends that the felt sense in my dream matched with one Chinese character in my daughter's name,

Ching (澄) – a word that means clarity and limpidness, Cliff grinned and asked, "Don't you know the Dharma Name of Master Thich Nhat Hanh is Ching Kong? (澄光 in Chinese)" – literally, light of limpidness (Trung Quang, in Vietnamese). I knew the master only by Thich Nhat Hanh, and had never heard of his other name Ching Kong.

When I went back to the dream with these two Chinese characters, I had a strong felt sense of clarity, of peace at heart, the limpid light deep within me. In this spiritual condition I could see through the maneuverings of the ego, tame violence, and reconcile confrontations. In Focusing terminology, "limpid light" was the handle to my felt sense. The wording matched my feeling and bodily sensations. I got the handle. The key was not the specific act of practicing mindfulness but the limpid light that shone through the heart.

The first part of the dream was the social-vs-spiritual debate, the second part was the life-saving redemption of the animals. The two parts were ingeniously integrated, with the first part symbolized by the second; the teaching of peace was played out in the saving of the animals and in the sacrifice of the lamb. The first part, like a tutorial in university, had lots of wordy discussion; the second was a theatrical performance without dialogue. The two parts were bridged by Frank, who was blocking the opening. In real life, he is a professor well known for his clear and rational deliberation of abstract concepts. In the dream, I pulled him and the chair he was sitting on out of the way, so that the guiding light could shine through and the animals could get into the village. Only now could I see the symbolism in this small part of the dream. Frank was the projection of my rational and analytic self. Spiritual opening is beyond rationality. Clearing the blockage of the mind would let the limpid light shine through the heart.

Right after the Zoom meeting I went to the pavilion to open my mailbox. Liz's postcard was sitting at the bottom of a pile of letters. "We brought you to this retreat, '*Now we have a path. We have nothing to fear*.' We wish you enjoyment and inspiration." Liz and Cliff.

On the postcard, at the right-hand corner, the Zen master's seal was stamped there, in Chinese characters, ????, Nhat Hanh, Limpid Light.

Dreamwork: Moving Forward

We met a second time to follow up on the Plum Village dream. Cliff was perceptive. He was a bit worried about the dogs getting into the village. He reminded me of yet another delicate co-existence in my dream: lambs seemed pure, and dogs were unpredictable – loyal friends or self-serving foes? I hadn't differentiated dogs from lambs before, but when I looked into them again I noticed that I had compassion towards the lambs and some reservations about the dogs.

Ed was insightful, speaking with a smile, "Both the lambs and the dogs have been saved. In my Catholic conviction, the Heavenly Father shows mercy to all." This rang a bell in me. Yes, that is what the Gospels say. Jesus opens his arms to prostitutes, to the blind, the handicapped, and all those who are suffering. We don't have to assume that all the participants at the Plum Village retreat are "good". On the contrary, those entangled by rage, jealousy, and earthly longings are exactly the kind of people who would benefit from the teaching of mindfulness. Jesus saves the righteous as well as the corrupt. This is what the monks and nuns are doing, taking care of those in need, not checking whether the lambs are more deserving of redemption than the dogs.

Liz asked, "What kind of inner process has been manifested in your dream? What's a way of moving forward?" Yes, I could have thought up some "action plans", like visiting Plum Village for real ... But instead of analyzing my next steps, I would do better to pay more attention to my felt senses, the realm where dreams work best.

Liz's questions had been on my mind, reminding me to follow up on my dream. After the two Zoom meetings I reserved time for meditation. I didn't expect anything significant, but a short while into the meditation I started to have a very strong sensation of somatic flows, the heaviness of my limbs, the heightened awareness of my whole body bathing in a pool of energy. I had a visceral compassion for the dying lamb, I could feel its pulses, its narrow escape from the mass killing at the feast and its disoriented pilgrimage to Plum Village... Limpid light, soft and comforting, flowing through me. I considered the lifespan of the lamb in a flash, like a fish flipping its tail in the stream – the ending of a life was not an ending, its life was joyous and precious. I was in a peaceful and calm state, being here, being with other life forms, the lambs, the dogs, the monks, the nuns, and many of my friends – Peggy, Cliff, Ed, and Liz. Here we were, in a buoyant mood, moving effortlessly in the here and now.

In the dream, the lambs and the dogs were being rescued. In my meditation, I was also being rescued in Plum Village; protected, I was being taken care of. I didn't need to worry. Plum Village, in France and also in the hearts and minds of many, is a refuge and a spiritual home. There is indeed something for me to consider: to interpret this energy, to experience the redemption, to stroll around the far corners of Plum Village, to explore the trails in the hills, the valleys and the woods, following the limpid light, and to share my journey with all those who find their way to this sacred land. And, most importantly, the lamb as a symbol – at the heart of the Christian faith – is Christ's sacrifice and atonement for humanity. The image of the lamb has always been in my mind. Now almost a year after the dream in which the sacrificial lamb first appeared, the imagery reappeared in this Plum Village dream and brings with it new experiences and meanings.

Dreamwork: The Shameful Me and Cheerful Me

Constance had a lot of dreams yesterday, most of which sank into obscurity, but one scene stood out:

It is a hot sunny day. She is walking up the stairs of a big stadium towards the private-box seated area. Wondering why she got invited to this luxurious and privileged seating, she is surprised to find that up at the far end of the stairs stands Millie Bobby Brown, who starred in the Netflix TV series *Stranger Things* – her head shaved, dressed casually in T-shirt and jeans as her TV character, Eleven. Constance is even more surprised when Millie welcomes her with great enthusiasm, shouting her name from afar, running towards her and giving her a big hug. They draw the attention of the crowd immediately. Millie escorts Constance into their private room, chatting cheerfully along the way.

We had done quite a lot of dreamwork together and Constance was quick to recall the details of her sensations and feelings in the dream. The most distinct was the smell of marshmallow sweetness when they hugged, of Millie's perfume. Constance said that that was the first time her dream had had such an olfactory sensation. It was this distinct smell that kept the scene alive in her memory.

In the dream, Millie was cheerful. Constance, however, felt ashamed because she was sweating and thought she smelled bad. The attention of the people around them made her very uncomfortable. She thought that people would notice her body odor and she had nowhere to hide. Under the scorching sun, sweat had dried into a thin layer of salt at the back of her neck. She could recall the grainy sensation when she tried to tidy herself up.

There were many layers of suppressed emotions behind the overwhelming shame in her narrative. To break through the "tyranny" of waking rationality, dreams are often expressed in a language we won't use in our everyday lives. Millie Bobby

Brown is such a bold and shiny symbol by which the dream is trying to break through Constance's defense mechanism of shame and guilt. The star shines. She smells great. Her charm is infectious, and her fondness for Constance is not a pretense. There must be something more in the dream besides shame.

In IFS therapy Constance's shame narrative is a "*protector*". *Protectors* are a category of subpersonalities which have taken on specific roles with the intention of safeguarding the person from perceived threats. Constance has a *protector,* always shaming her as a way of motivating her to perform, trampling on her self-esteem, and obliterating her expectation as a way to avoid disappointment. I have known of this *protector* since Constance started talking to me about her depression, years ago. Both of us know very well the patterns of shame in her reactions to different life situations.

At first, the voice of this *protector* was masked by an array of distress and anxiety. After a long process of therapeutic intervention, the voice and emotive reactions of this *protector* have become much more distinguishable.

Despite the shiny aura of the dream, Constance was using yet again the narrative of shame. I asked her to ground herself, close her eyes and get back to the dream scene. I asked her to be friendly to this *protector* and let him take a back seat, then walk up the stairs again really slowly, and let her feelings, if any, come up. Now she had the space to allow some unfamiliar feelings to emerge. She was curious about why a well-known star was being friendly to her. She felt honored to be recognized, happy to be taken seriously...

At this point, I asked Constance to pause a bit and slow down. "Stay there. Sense fully that happy feeling..." In her waking life she hates being the center of attention, she keeps away from photo-taking occasions in gatherings and ceremonies, and she always sneaks away from parties. Now, as she re-experienced her dream, she reacted as many normal people would do, feeling honored and happy in a situation like this one. "Yes, I feel happy, despite the feeling of shame…" she said.

In her dream, she was sweaty, I asked her to "scan" Millie's reactions when they hugged each other. "Does she look awkward or uneasy?"

Constance, "Not at all."

"Is your shame there?"

"Yes."

"Does Millie notice your sweatiness?"

"Yes."

"So, you can simultaneously feel the shame as well as the good feeling of being accepted and befriended by Millie?"

"Yes."

In real life, the star is criticized for wearing too much make-up. In the dream, she dressed down, very much in line with Constance. They were just like two regular youngsters enjoying themselves.

Re-experiencing the dream made Constance feel very comfortable, especially in such a luxe setting in which guests were supposed to dress up.

After a while, I asked Constance to walk through the whole scene from Millie's point of view. In the dream, Millie was not the actual actress; instead, she was a symbol constructed out of Constance's inner resources. Now Millie was looking at Constance, the dream ego, from the other end of the stairs. "I am so excited to see Constance, I love to spend time with her like other girls do. The crowd is looking at us, but they don't matter a bit. I am determined to ignore all the attention and enjoy my time with Constance."

I asked, "Constance is sweaty, don't you mind?"

"Not at all, we are all sweating like hell while filming outdoors."

Now Constance had the embodied experience from Millie's perspective. Yes, actors and actresses are accustomed to outdoor filming under the unforgiving sun. Knowing that, I asked her to walk up those stairs again one more time and feel the difference. With dual-awareness, Constance paid more attention to how Millie felt, and the time spent with Millie was much more pleasant and intimate.

In her waking life Constance is accustomed to avoiding others' attention. It is a feeling so real and genuine that she thinks it is innate to her personality. She even has trouble looking at her own photos. I reminded her that all through her childhood she was a natural leader among her peers. She published a novel at the age of 12 and instantly became the star student in her primary school. Her world was turned upside down when she was transferred to the high school with the super-rich kids. In her own words, she had fallen to being the lowest of the food chain. That was the moment when her *protector* had gathered strength and become a dominant part of her character. In the first few months in that international school, she quickly learned a few lessons: catching attention was undesirable; she shouldn't have any expectation of being recognized; laying low would help her stay away from contempt and bullying...

Her shame had gradually taken the driver's seat of her daily life to become the matter-of-fact master, whereas her star quality turned dull and dormant. Ironically, her original charismatic and cheerful personality has become a child in exile, hidden in a remote corner of her grown-up life. Now in the twilight of her recovery, this exile was trying to re-emerge in the form of Constance's opposite, Eleven, the radiant character in one of her favorite drama series. Constance is not yet ready to welcome and embrace the return of the confident, charismatic character she once was, but Millie, the pop star, shone through the dream. Her aura filled up the scene, whereas the *protector*, with all its (his?)

shame on her shoulders, couldn't undo Millie's enthusiasm. I have confidence that one day, Eleven, the cheerful one, will get back into the driver's seat with a more compassionate heart, for Constance has been living in shadow, she knows what it is like to be inside the dark tunnel, and she will have a more empathic understanding of how to be a happy, considerate, and caring person.

Chapter 7

The Wool Ball, the Smelly Cat, and the Cranky Corpse

Eating Disorder, an Enigma

An Eating Disorder (ED) is a complex, intricate, and sticky illness that involves the whole family in years of torment. Recovery is slow, with intermittent relapses. There is a strange in-group/out-group boundary between families with an ED member and those without. From the outside, the pain and suffering are difficult to comprehend. The illness seems to be a disorder of mere eating, not a serious kind of illness such as cancer. However, the illness draws everybody in the family into emotional turmoil. The dining table becomes a battleground, triggering rage and despair daily, lasting for years.

The symptoms of ED vary from restricting food intake, over-exercising, binge-eating and induced vomiting, to deadly self-starvation, or compulsive over-eating. Besides these observable physical symptoms, every ED patient is deeply afflicted with a cluster of emotional disorders like obsessive-compulsive disorder, depression, anxiety, panic attacks, self-harm, insomnia, and a seriously distorted perception of weight and body shape. Added to these physical and psychological complications, ED is also a reflection of dysfunctional communication in the family, which usually involves the parents. The illness is not just inside the body and mind of the patient, but intricately linked to a web stubbornly rooted in family history.

It is estimated that about one-third of patients will reach full recovery. Another third will have some symptoms for the rest of their lives. And about 30% will remain severely ill, usually dying far younger than they should.

For more than seven years, Teresa and I have attended a monthly gathering of the parent support group for ED kids. Newcomers are eager to find ways to fix the problems of their loved ones, but often old-hands will share their experiences, having found that making effective changes to themselves are the best way to help, rather than making direct efforts at "fixing" the child.

In a recent meeting, Sally's account touched the hearts of old and new alike. Her daughter Zoe became ill six years ago when she was in high school. Typical of most ED patients, Zoe was a gifted high-achiever, sensitive, perfectionist, and an obedient child. A bright child is the pride of the parents, but when illness breaks out the family is thrown into chaos. Sally had gone through the emotional pain of seeing Zoe's deterioration – hair falling out, the stopping of her menstruation, her BMI dropping to a life-threatening level, tube-feeding, hospitalization, relapses, and a failed suicide attempt... Sally's lips quivered as she recalled the sickening ordeals.

Like most parents, Sally put a lot of effort into finding ways to force Zoe to eat, more often than not to no avail. In despair Sally ended up seeing a clinical psychologist herself, and things started to change with her insight and self-awareness. She had been a dominant mother throughout, taking command of every family decision. They lived with Sally's father, who, unsurprisingly was also a dominant character. Sally gradually came to the realization that in the family, she and her father would do almost all the talking. Everybody else stayed silent all the time. No one talked back.

Sally knew she was part of the problem. It was difficult for her to change her life-long habit of dealing with things, but she tried hard. Gradually, relations between Sally and the other members of the family started to change, and so did Zoe's health.

Sally told the parents in the group, "To cut a long story short, I learned a few things in those testing years. The first lesson is to stop giving advice all the time. Listen with an open mind, and especially with a sympathetic heart. To always provide solutions to your daughter is counterproductive. You will give a lot to your family just by listening and doing nothing. Zoe gets a lot of love and care when I lend her my ears.

"Another thing I learned at a much later stage is not to expect a 'full recovery'. Zoe is still exercising two hours a day and she still follows a restrictive diet. But she is happy and is able to cope with stress in her life. That's good enough for me.

"And don't be surprised if your loved one relapses. Life is full of challenges. Zoe might face yet another difficulty that she can't resolve. She might fall back on her strict diet as an escape. As long as there is love and bonding between us, it is good enough.

"And finally, in hindsight, I see these strenuous years as a blessing. My family life has changed a lot. We're much happier than before."

Sally's words resonated in me in a profound way, for I have learned the same hard-earned lessons too. As I listened to her story, I felt as if I was witnessing Constance's story projected on a movie screen.

Sally's "happy ending" is in direct contrast with Joyce's heartbreaking story. It is misleading to paint a rosy scenario of recovery without pointing out the dark side of this baffling disorder. Full recovery is difficult to achieve. An eating disorder is malicious. It is as nasty, if not more severe, as the most difficult psychiatric illness of the day.

Joyce's daughter had a history of self-starvation. The week previous to the time of writing, Joyce's Daughter, having refused to eat for many days, passed away on the way to the hospital. The news was devastating to Teresa and me. We had both been with Joyce for several years, fighting the monster in her daughter's life. And the battle was lost.

We understand how it feels. It reminds us all in the parent caring group that an eating disorder is double-edged. It can be healed and bring about changes for the whole family, but it hurts and can bring irredeemable loss.

Teresa and I knew it would do no good to tell Constance the sad story, and we agreed not to tell her. But strangely, out of the blue, and never having met her, she brought her up, asking, "How is Joyce?"

I hesitated, but then I told her all we knew. I didn't want to hide. And I was curious about how Constance had come to ask about her at that moment. She didn't know about the tragedy. For more than half a year she hadn't asked about any specific person in the parent group.

She told me that she had had a strong sense of Joyce being in severe pain. That was why she asked. Joyce was, indeed, in extreme pain after losing her daughter in such an abrupt way. To us this was another confirmation that Constance has a psychic sensitivity to things concerning life and death.

The Malicious Impulses

Once a month I go with Constance to see her psychiatrist, Dr. Wang, who listens to her update and invites me to make any observations on the progress she's making. In a recent consultation Constance brought up the old issue of her sensory sensitivity, which has diminished since she started taking some psychotropic drugs Dr. Wang prescribed for her three years ago. The change was quite abrupt as she felt it right away. At that time, disoriented, she didn't have the mental strength to make sense of these intriguing changes. Now, after almost three years of recovery, she recalled that in the first few months after taking the drug, it was a shock when her world of sound and sight suddenly changed.

In her whole life before this, color was rich, sound was sharp, memory was photographic. But after taking the pills everything literally turned pale. The bold colors of Van Gogh faded into the impressionism of Monet. The fact that she can remember tiny details has always amazed her friends. She is able to tell others what clothes they were wearing the first time they met, years ago. Now she still amazes her friends, serving as their instant Wikipedia for who's who in politics, tech news, showbiz, and especially in films. But her ability to memorize trivia has been hampered by the drugs. She feels sad for the loss to this day.

Dr. Wang explained why Constance had these psychological changes. She told us that Constance was born with the gift of an amplified sensory capacity. For instance, her photographic memory might be a consequence of her intensified vision leaving an imprint of everything she sees. With these enhanced abilities, there are pros and cons – Van Gogh painted in shocking colors that normal people couldn't see, but he cut his ear off when he became delusional.

When incoming sensory signals are too overwhelming, Constance suffers from sensory overload, and she has accepted this abnormality as a basic fact of life. This is the world she has known since her birth. Constance had told me many times that she was afraid of certain specific sounds and sights, like the scraping of metal, and the inky tides of the sea at night. Now that these heightened sensitivities have been adjusted by chemical means, Dr. Wang explained, there is a sense of loss, of something missing, but there are also benefits in the lessening of anxiety and relieving the mind of its heavy workload. As the dosage is gradually tuned down, Constance will one day be capable of adjusting her sensory reception to a comfortable level, not by using chemicals, but by the regulatory mechanism in herself.

After this consultation, we had an interesting conversation on our evening walk, where we touched on issues we felt might not have been appropriate in the clinical setting of Dr. Wang's office. I asked Constance what else, other than hypersensitivity, was in the "package" she had been given. I knew about the flashes of violent images that had flooded her at times since her childhood, and that these images had receded as she grew older and had stopped altogether when she graduated from high school.

As we walked, she said a little more about those now obsolete experiences. Only now was I starting to fully realize how serious her sufferings have been since her birth as she described the sudden impulses involving hurting people around her and "witnessing" the brutal consequences of what she might have done in vivid and gruesome detail.

For instance, standing on the platform with her classmate, waiting for the train to pull in, she would suddenly have the impulse to push her friend onto the rails. Then would come the vivid, fast-forwarded image of the train hitting the body. She would stand, one hand clutching the other, forbidding the carrying out of the impulse, while her normal self, deep inside, was screaming in great fear. But she would act calmly, as if nothing was happening. This kind of drama would play out almost every day. Almost everyone she loved was on the hit list, which continues to trigger intense guilt and shame up to the present day.

I asked, "Were those images hazy?"

"No. They were real, very real."

"Were you forced to act them out?"

"The impulses were not that forceful, but I had to hold my hands together firmly, or step back."

"Did they flood in without any triggers?"

Constance replied, "Usually whenever I saw sharp objects like knives and scissors, or heard shrieking sounds, like someone dragging a chair or cutting a piece of steak on a ceramic plate, these impulses would surge in."

Shaken, I said, "You never told us any of this when you were young. To us, you were a happy child."

"I knew the thought of killing or hurting someone was terribly bad. I kept my secret in my heart."

"Would they be images that came from movies or story books?" I wondered.

"No. They were there as far back as I can remember..."

With these details, I could imagine how painful it was for Constance, as just a little child, to keep the secret and bear the guilt all by herself. To have those vivid and graphic images manifest... I guess there must have been a violent subpersonality actively turning intentions into visual reality. In counter-balancing these malicious impulses, there was obviously an equally powerful determination in the frightened child, to disapprove of and inhibit the intended crimes. This violent part of Constance was given to her, she didn't have a choice.

These dramas gradually became less frequent and at a certain point they disappeared for good, but Constance still has to deal with her guilt, which nags at her all the time in a harsh voice.

I wondered where that violent subpersonality came from, and why had it faded out? Was it an inborn neurobiological structure that had degenerated over the years? Or was it the residue of another violent being? Was it a template which had not been wiped clean, so that Constance couldn't start anew?

Together we came up with another more "mainstream" explanation: as her sensory perception was so acute and much amplified ever since birth, it may well have trapped a lot of stress and anxiety inside her. Those violent impulses and images could well be a form of release. However, given that it all started when Constance was very young, how could she, an infant, have cooked up such images from scratch? Where did those violent images come from?

It's clear that Constance was born with the ability to vaguely connect with people from other worlds. For instance, in an Airbnb in Japan she had felt threatened by an old lady there, and later found, looking in archive news, the image of the same landlady who had died in the house. And, some years ago, my sister had wanted to buy an apartment in K-Town but was suspicious because of the exceptionally low price. She invited us to take a look around. Without any previous knowledge of the apartment, Constance felt the presence of the old lady owner of the flat. We later found out that the old lady had passed away inside the apartment, and not in a peaceful way. My sister didn't make the purchase.

Now, Constance's psychic sensitivity has been dampened, which I think is good for her.

As we plumbed her childhood memory, she reminded me of something I had forgotten. When she was seven she was scared by a blue silhouette outside her bedroom window, so she slept on the floor of our room for almost a year. I had completely forgotten about this. At that time, I had dismissed the episode as a mere stress related fantasy. Now I wanted her to say more. She recalled that the silhouette was a hazy figure, in luminous blue; it had the form of a man, in some way nasty (she didn't know how she got that, she just knew he was a nasty person). What scared her was that the figure was aware that she had noticed him, and that the mutual noticing seemed to expose her to the scowling of a hostile being.

I should have taken this more seriously. Constance's suffering was much more severe than I had thought. If she is receptive to spiritual interferences the violent images in her young mind might have come from outside of her. However, I don't want to dwell on this realm unknown to me. It is enough to let her experiences speak. I am more empathic now. I fully acknowledge the suffering she has endured. What remains to be done is to help Constance free herself from the guilt of her intriguing past.

The Healing Power of the Mother Tree

Brian, Teresa, and I attended the reunion of the *Self-Care in Nature* Program on the day, according to the Chinese traditional calendar, known as "the great heat". We were a group of twelve who took a tour at Karrie Farm, a near-150 hectare conservation area encompassing valleys, streams, creeks, and lush woodlands. In contrast to the heat of the unforgiving sun in the city, the woodlands were cool and refreshing. Running streams and waterfalls served as natural air-conditioners puffing misty breezes into the air. It was comfortable walking along the winding trails through the shrubs and groves, sheltered by giant trees and cascades of king-sized ferns.

Resting on the trunks and branches were bird's nest ferns, which conspicuously spread their blade-shaped leaves like fountains. The trees simply provide the fern spores with a space to flourish. The sprouting ferns gather moisture and fallen leaves from the air, precipitating piles of humus like a bird's nest, and live harmoniously with the hosts. These ferns burgeoned all over the valleys, a pronounced symbol of the loving generosity of the giving trees.

Throughout the five-hour trip, PH, our tutor, led us to a variety of trees so that we could discern the differences in the types of energy they were emitting. All these trees have been around for many years and are generous in giving care to other fellow beings. Different in their physique and "temperament", some are motherly, some are energetic and fiery.

Comparing and contrasting sharpened our sensitivity towards the different forms of energy in nature. For instance, there was a pathway named the "energy gate", where two big fragrant maples stood side by side, like the two vertical frames of a door. When we walked past the gate or stood in the middle, we could sense a rhythmic vibration. As PH explained, the two trees were sending out energy waves toward each other, and we in the middle could sense their interactive pulses.

Before lunch, we greeted a mother camphor tree standing at the center of a valley. Her gigantic branches spread evenly in all directions, her impressive crown sheltered the understory of ferns and thickets. Bird's nest ferns rested on her branches. Many of us instantly felt her caring embrace, as if she was holding us peacefully in her arms. We felt safe and protected. When I put my hands on her trunk, my palms had a distinctive throbbing sensation. Sometimes it takes a while for me to garner a connection with trees. In many instances, I don't feel a thing at all. But this mother tree standing before me was very generous. Readily available was a natural flow of energy from the tree to all of us. PH said we could ask the tree to share her healing power. Constance came to my mind and I wondered if the healing power of the mother tree could do some good for her recovery.

Last week, while she was Focusing with me, Constance recalled three dreadful images from her deep depression a few years back. At that time we were taking stock of the signposts of recovery we had gone through together.

The first scene was of a sick kitten, soaking wet, inside a dark and smelly sewage ditch. The feeble cat was hiding in the dark and afraid of light. Constance even had a sensation of being burnt when beams of light, in her mind, shone through the ditch.

The second image was a messy ball of wool in her chest, wet and sticky, with decaying pustules oozing blood, thick and dark. This image came up quite often when she was in suffocating mode. The foul ball was entangled with dead knots and sometimes it would swell up to the verge of bursting.

In the third scene, Constance fell off a crag and landed on a small rock platform where a corpse lay on a ledge. The corpse clutched her arm and talked to her in a squeaky voice. Constance could see and smell the decaying body, rotten to the bone. Despite her intense fear, she didn't push him off the ledge. She felt sympathy for him.

These three scenes have stuck in both our minds, reminding us of the desperation of being inside the dark tunnel with the end nowhere in sight. When they emerged at different points over the past seven years, the images were accompanied by intense somatic reactions. I remember when the wool ball first appeared, Constance was short of breath as she uttered in pain that her chest was going to burst. Now, as she has been recovering, these distressing images are dormant and no longer haunt her daily life.

As I stood contemplatively by the hillside, these images came to me again and I wondered whether Constance could benefit from the healing power of the mother tree.

There were two hitches: firstly, she was not here. Could I relay the healing power to her from afar? And secondly, these images were from the past. Constance had already gone through those terrible stages despite their stickiness in her mind. The images were no longer embodied in the somatic conditions of her depression. They were no longer bundled with the sickness; would there be any cleansing effects if I brought them up again?

After lunch, we had half an hour of individual free time to find a companion tree nearby. Going back to the mother tree, I wanted to try cleansing those sticky images in my memory, but I wasn't sure I knew how to proceed. After a few unsuccessful tries, I dropped the idea of dealing with the imagery. The group joined up again at Covent Garden, where we started to descend the hill along a stream.

Beside a small waterfall we took a break to enjoy the burbling sound echoing on the rocks and boulders of the gullies. In a spontaneous move, PH invited us to close our eyes in front of the waterfall, mindfully breathing in and exhaling the stresses we accumulated from our busy lives.

This was a peaceful moment given to me out of the blue. The images came up again automatically, sticky and vivid. This alone was reason enough for me to give them a cleansing. It didn't matter whether they were outdated or not, they were still unprocessed.

With my eyes closed, first came the wool ball, sickening and decaying. I should have done something to it a long time ago. In deep contemplation, I put it under the waterfall. The gentle rinsing in the running water was refreshing, gradually washing off the thick pus and blood. The dark color of the coils of wool faded away and the original pastel color reappeared, the dead knots were straightened out, and the wool ball became soft and fluffy again.

The stinky sick cat was hesitant, but Mother Nature was caring and welcoming. The glittering stream brought into the dark ditch fresh air and bright sunlight. I visualized the cat slowly walking out of the darkness, getting cleaned up, and perching on a big rock beside the waterfall, enjoying the sun. The furry cat was dry and clean. I felt great for her.

I had trouble dealing with the corpse, I didn't have an image of his face, the details were fleeting ... So, I left it at that.

Our next stop was the Cascade Garden, a lovely circular glade with a big hackberry tree towering over the open space. On the ground was a fish mosaic, paved in small ceramic tiles of pastel green, pink, yellow, and blue. We stayed in front of the hackberry for a quiet time. Continuing with my visualization, the wool ball loosened up to become a very long curly thread. Little by little it knitted itself into a colorful embroidery of a fish. The cat was sitting under the tree, calm and healthy, kitten no more, she was now a grown-up companion cat. The corpse had regenerated a bit but was still insubstantial and shadowy, without a face.

The last stop was another camphor tree, big, tall, and standing upright – PH called it the "father tree". His energy was different, giving us a firm and stable sensation. Under this father tree, the adult cat became more energetic, jumping onto a branch in a swift and agile movement. More interestingly, the corpse transformed to become a normal man. His face was still vague to me, but he could stand and walk freely. He left, vanished into the woodland, freeing himself from Constance's dreadful past. I felt good for him. I suddenly realized that the wool ball and the cat were parts of Constance, but the corpse was not. It was her sick condition rather than an integral part of her.

As we came close to the end of the trip, the uncomfortable feelings attached to the sticky wool ball and sick cat were gone. I was delighted. Little by little, the cleansing rituals had added up. The fish embroidery and the companion cat were now dear to my heart, and the new images stayed with me. I didn't know whether these cleansings and healings were having an effect on Constance, but the healing power of the giving trees, the revitalizing stream, the lively woodlands, and the peaceful gardens had relieved my burdens and renewed my understanding of my daughter's recovery.

Time Is Flexible

I didn't tell Constance about what had happened at Karrie, I just asked her to do something about those three images she had recalled a few days ago. I invited her to imagine what the wool ball, the sick cat and the corpse might be like after all these years. The following day she told me that, in her contemplations, some things had happened to the wool ball and the sick cat. It could also be described as Jung's active imagination, which I have practiced with her for a few years. She has a gift for visualizing feeling and the internal felt sense.

In her imagination, she went back to Southampton, where we had stayed for a year in 1993. At that time, Constance was a five-year-old child, Teresa was taking a Masters program at

Southampton University, while I was doing my PhD thesis at London University. Our landlady Mrs. Marche, who was then in her 70s, made a knitted doll for Constance. In Constance's mind, the sickening wool ball was that doll, wet and sticky.

Mrs. Marche was sitting beside the bathtub in our Southampton home, cleaning some stains on the doll. Constance, a naughty little girl at that time, was bathing in the murky water. She didn't mind sharing the bathtub with that stinky doll. Mrs. Marche managed to clean up both of them. Constance was bossy and forced Mrs. Marche to blow dry her hair first, the wet doll had to wait for its turn. Since the wool was just one pale color, Mrs. Marche knitted a hat in vivid orange for the doll, which looked like a lively little strawman. Now both were clean and tidy. Mrs. Marche said gently, "You guys can be good buddies."

Listening to Constance's recounting, I was glad to hear that this cleansing ritual was accomplished in Southampton, where Constance enjoyed one of the happiest years in her life. She then told me about her cleansing of the cat:

Right from the beginning, the sick cat was already in the bathroom of our home in K-Town. Next to it was Charcoal, our beloved cat, cheering the poor one up. The cleaning process was nasty. There were worms, dirt, and smelly discharges all over her body. Because of the hard rubbing and rinsing the cat was uncomfortable and occasionally hissed in pain. But she knew it was good for her. The cat ended up neat and tidy, resting comfortably in the living room. With all the dirt gone, Constance could see the smart grey stripes on this tabby cat. The transformation was obvious, and the cat is now a member of the family.

Relatively speaking, the cleansing of the knitted doll and the cat were straightforward. As for the dead guy, Constance found it difficult to process. She gave up.

It was as far back as 2015 when the corpse came up in a Focusing session she'd had, led by Edwin, the experienced trainer from my Focusing class. She had first told me of her condition around this time, so I invited her to try a session of Focusing to see whether it would help. Back then, after her first experience with Focusing, Constance didn't tell me any details as I drove her home. She just said she hated Focusing. Images and sensations kept rushing and hustling. Things were out of control, and the corpse was frenetic, begging for help in one moment, and in the next, threatening to do harm to her.

It had been many years since the corpse first appeared, but it was still in Constance's mind. For my part, I was delighted to see the dead man leaving me at Karrie, but I was not sure how the dead man would transform for Constance. Anyhow, now the knitted strawman is cute, and the cat is lovely. I hoped she would soon find closure over the dreadful image of the dead man.

These rituals lead me to ponder some tricky issues concerning time and space. Constance was dealing with her cleansing without any knowledge of what I had done at Karrie. However, despite some variations, there are notable similarities, especially in her knitted doll and my fish embroidery, and the problematic nature of dealing with the corpse. I can certainly think of some reasons behind these overlaps. I share her healing history and I have a deep concern about her health. Except for the scene of the corpse, which came to her with Edwin as her listener, the other two arose from the Focusing sessions she did with me. The wool ball and the sick cat are deep in her emotive memory, and in mine as well. The good intention of cleansing would surely induce a similar process of transformation in each of our minds.

To me, time seems to be flexible in the sequence of events. The three scenes are buried in the past, yet Constance recalled them a few days before my Karrie trip, where they popped up again in my mind and triggered the cleansing rituals. Constance did hers a day later, echoing what I had done in a different time and place. I am not sure whether this could be seen as a case of synchronicity. Certainly, it is meaningful to each of us, but is it an instance of non-causal coincidence? There are altogether four happenings, first, Constance's recall of the images; second, my Karrie trip; third, my cleansing rituals; fourth, Constance's cleansing rituals. There are no direct causal relations in between; one doesn't cause the happening of the other, apart from the fourth one, where I did ask her to do something about the images.

But of course, there was a strong intentionality shooting through the entire sequence of events. Constance's full recovery is very much hoped for, and especially by me. Our intentions have motivated the cleansing rituals, thus they are not entirely random. But these synchronistic events have some beneficial effects on both of us, and the whole experience has juxtaposed the past and present of her recovery process in a way that is beyond our imagination.

Meeting the Future Me

Is it possible for Constance and me, in the present, to transmit our blessing to the Constance and me of the past, at the time when we were inside the dark tunnel of depression? A long question. Or simply put, can we talk to our past? Can I tell the me of the past that things have already been changed for the better? If yes, what would the effects of that be?

Cognitive neuro-scientist Julia Mossbridge has recorded her own precognitive dreams and visions as well as those of many others. She once received a message from her future self, telling her that her sick boyfriend had recovered and was *now* in robust health. The message came at a time when he was gravely ill. His lungs were deteriorating to the point of no return. Then the message from her future came true. He had a lung transplant and now he is, indeed, in robust health. In another incident, she had an urge to check out whether the garage door was locked, and by doing so, prevented a fire that would have ignited his boyfriend's oxygen tank. She writes, "It was as if the future had reached out, gently pulled me forward, and showed me what needed to be done."

Theresa Cheung, a spiritual writer and a well-known dream expert, co-authored with Mossbridge the book *The Premonition Code,* in which she wrote about an important dream at the beginning of her writing career. She dreamed about choosing a turn in the wilderness, her late mother called her name and told her to "take the right path". According to Cheung, the dream was as vivid as watching a movie. The next day, she was driving in great haste to an interview. At a junction, when she was about to turn left, her dream flashed into her mind, and she made a quick decision to turn right, and later found out that by turning right, she avoided a fatal car accident. The dream at night penetrated time, playing out in the next day.

In theoretical physics, it is a consensus that time and space are relative. When physicists play with formulas in relativity, the time vector can be either positive or negative, while in our everyday experiences time can only move forward. We can remember the past but not the future, which is not yet actualized and can't be perceived from the vantage point of the present. In their co-authored book, Cheung and Mossbridge challenge this linear and unidirectional conception of time. They argue that time is flexible, and we can "remember" the future, only that this capacity has been inhibited by the modern and rational mind. I will not get into the debate here and will leave open the analytic arguments. Instead, I will share the following precognitive experience in a phenomenological manner, bracketing the questions of the why and the how, judgements and beliefs.

Let me write in the present tense a moment-by-moment description:

Following a guided meditative ritual, I am lying on my bed with my eyes closed. I am invited to imagine a scene from which

I start a journey. From several options in my memory, I choose a memorable scene at the end of one of my dreams, in which I am standing on a train platform with a sacrificial lamb in my arms. I am embarking on a journey unknown to me.

This is the dream I had last year, which ended on the platform. In my meditation I am being invited to meet the future me, two or five years from now maybe, but for quite a while nothing is happening. The platform is still empty. The scene is other-worldly, bright, clean, and neat, as it was in the dream.

Some imaginative futures pop up in my mind. There's a guy walking towards me with a pair of handcuffs hanging from his belt, triggering my fear. In a split second the scene changes. I am standing in a brightly lit hall, hearing a voice telling me that I will be OK and won't be thrown in jail.

Are these precognitions? I doubt it. Swinging back and forth are these speculative scenarios, the worst and the most desirable. They seem to have arisen from my fear and the desire of my active mind in the present.

Leaving these speculations behind, I go back to mindfully attending to the sensations in my torso, then the tingling fingers, arms, legs… Gradually, I have an awareness of my body, a tangible sensation, luminously morphing. Suddenly this sensation doubles up. It's as if my awareness is being dialed up, amplified. My body is becoming more "substantial". I am pondering, "Is the future me doubling up with the present me? Am I making this up?" In my analytic mind, I am not sure of the answers, but I am quite certain that my awareness has been "thickened". This is more of a somatic confirmation than a cognitive knowing. It is a felt sense that I am not being targeted in the case of financial dispute. I am a loving father to Constance and a loving husband to Teresa. The three of us are close, hearts and minds together. My book has been published and read by those who are suffering. I can't see the readers, but I can see the flipping of the pages.

The double meaning of the I Ching verse – maiden coming back/getting married – both come true. My daughter is Fred's wife. She has recovered. She has come back. The present me is in awe because Constance doesn't want to get married. It is too much pressure for her. She won't allow it to happen. I am in great doubt. Interestingly, I am simultaneously having the feeling of the future me, bringing a very real felt sense of contentment, happy about her marriage, without any surprise at all. In the future, her marriage is a fact. No surprise.

The Plum Village dream comes up again. The present me is uncertain about the meaning of the dying lamb. The feeling of perplexity is here, but at the same time I know as a fact that I am the one who is offering the lamb as a sacrifice for the people in the city. The lamb is peaceful, serving as a sacred sacrifice at the altar for the purpose of cleansing the violence and suffering of the secular world.

Again, there is a doubling up of two sensibilities. One is the perplexity of the present, the other is certainty in the future. In the dream, I carried a dead lamb on a train platform. In another more recent dream, the lamb was dying in front of me inside the sanctuary. Both dreams ended without closure. The present me doesn't know what is going to happen next. But for the future me, things are certain. I have a role to play, I am going to offer a lamb. My role as one who presents the peace offering is to share my gratitude and make a vow to facilitate compassion and kindness. This is the spiritual journey the present me is going to take, to facilitate compassion, to actualize the future.

I will leave these words above as they stand. I will revisit this passage sometime in the future to witness the unfolding of my precognitions. The cautious me would like to check whether the written statements will come true or not. But the existential me has no doubt about the precognition, so it will be the witnessing of the unfolding, not a checking the truth of the claim. Time will tell. Or the future has already spoken.

Closure for the Corpse

On our evening walk, I had a session of Focusing with Constance on her memory of the corpse. I was hesitant about it, for every time she talked about it, she felt a grave pull of horror. We needed an anchor, firm and safe, before visiting this dreadful scene again. We each grounded ourselves on the boardwalk by the sea, listening to the humming of the insects in the background and tuning in to our bodily sensations of the present moment.

I set the scene by imagining us riding bicycles up a hill. We had tried this a few years previously and Constance had found her mind full of sharp objects and the sound of rusty bicycle gears. This time, I deliberately changed the details and told her I had already polished the sharp edges of the gears so that her bicycle wouldn't make shrieking noises like before. She had imagined our cat Charcoal, her loving companion for many years, sitting comfortably in the front basket of her bicycle.

Having taken all these precautions, we arrived at the ledge where the corpse was lying. But there was no corpse! For me, the image was ambiguous. It was for Constance to explore the scene herself.

In her imagination, against the blue sky, a Japanese carp flag was flapping in a gentle breeze, and a gigantic airship floated in the air, the pilot smiling at us just like the Miyazaki Hayao animated film *The Wind Rises*. She described the scene to me as it unfolded. I felt it was safe since she had come up with such a bright and cheerful image, however, she started to recall the eerie feeling of the room where she had done the Focusing with Edwin in 2015.

With Charcoal in her arms, she revisited the corpse but could only see a hand, dry and bony, with blue veins all over it. The body of the corpse was in silhouette. She smelled decay too. Tension was building. A part of me was eager to say goodbye to all of this so that Constance could have closure. I didn't want the corpse to gather its evil force. But I held back my wish for her to push it away from her. I stayed with her, patiently waiting, loosening hold on my expectations.

All of a sudden, Constance smiled. In her imagination, she had become a cartoon character, *Emily the Strange*, and Charcoal had turned into a cartoon cat. In this famous cartoon series, Emily and her cat are both in their signature black while the background is always in shocking red. Interestingly, the scene split into two. The side with the corpse remained as real as a documentary, and the other side was a 2-Dimensional cartoon. On the corpse's side, it was graphic. On Constance's side, it was cartoonish black and red.

My hunch was that in revisiting this traumatic episode Constance was setting up a psychological fence to separate the horrific sickness and her recovering self. She was borrowing the "I don't give a damn" sarcastic persona of Emily to reverse the power relationship between the corpse and herself. In her own words, "Now Emily has the upper hand." The corpse's manipulative power was running out of steam. Emily was even spilling ketchup on the corpse. "Hey! Blood! Want more?"

I asked her, "What would Emily do next?"

Constance ranted, "Emily is bad, as always. She wants to burn the corpse."

"Ask Charcoal, what he would do?"

"Oh, Charcoal says no, don't be cruel." Then, with a flash of insight, Constance lowered her voice, "Emily tosses off a verse, 'Been here!' Then off she goes."

In Chinese, "been here" (到此一遊) is a four-character phrase that people would inscribe on a tree or a boulder to say *I visited this place*, then adding the day, month, and year. People don't do this anymore, so there's a nostalgic element to this way of saying goodbye.

There is a shift in Constance's re-experiencing of this most horrifying stage of her depression, she can fence off the past from the present, wittingly mobilizing the energies from a familiar cartoon character to deplete the manipulative power of the corpse. "Been here" is a touch of magic. On the surface, it is nothing more than an old-fashioned inscription, commonly seen in K-Town's countryside decades ago, but sinking deep into the latent meaning in this context, it is really a witty insight from the mysterious unconscious of Constance's recovering soma. It means closure and leaving. People write this and leave the scene. It marks that someone has been here – a memorable and meaningful moment not to be forgotten. It is nostalgic, something of the past, but life goes on. The decaying corpse was unbearable, but in the healing process, "been here" is a playful statement that the ordeal has already been endured, the bad no longer hurts, and the good is welcome.

Focusing and Active Imagination

Edwin, Liz and Cliff, all licensed trainers in Focusing, met with me via Zoom to discuss the series of cleansing rituals I had done with Constance. Our discussion touched on issues concerning Focusing, active imagination and healing. Focusing deals with the somatic felt sense, implicit emotions, imageries, and symbols beyond the rational control of the thinking mind. The late Eugene Gendlin said that they are the wisdom of the body which we can elicit from the *implicit*, a borderline realm between the conscious and the unconscious, in-between the known and the unknown. Focusing shares some parallels with Jung's active imagination, when the conscious me taps deep into the unconscious, looking for characters, images and symbols that will unfold, talk back, and inspire, in order to move towards greater self-awareness. Active imagination is done in solo meditation, while the standard Focusing practice is to have a listener echo what the Focuser feels. Despite the differences the logic is similar – to let the implicit imageries unfold and come alive. Active imagination may involve painting, creative writing, dancing etc., while Focusing can also be meditative or combined with expressive arts.

In the cleansing rituals Constance and I did over the past two weeks, the images and their transformation all had latent meanings, initially not clear to us. Images break through the strong grid of rationality. They bring with them complex, contradictory and even prohibited emotions. To Constance, the corpse was repulsive, evil and manipulative, but the dead man was sad, miserable and had a tragic history. She had sympathy for him and didn't want to add to his suffering by shaking him off.

Liz recognized the situation. She knew the feeling of getting stuck with a nasty and toxic friend and yet feeling obliged to stay and listen to him. Very similar to the way the corpse was coercing Constance. It would be a big temptation to help this friend out, but the sympathizer risks falling into the same messy entanglement of the sickened individual.

Constance's corpse is a graphic representation of her depression, with complicated feelings of dreadfulness, self-pity, and melancholic indulgence. And these mixed feelings are felt by many in life situations very different from hers. These images can tell a story full of contradictory emotions that won't be leveled out into a logical linearity. Imageries are far more energetic than words, they are polysemic, rich in meaning, expressing themselves both in Focusing and in active imagination.

With its protean plasticity, Jungian active imagination gives the Focuser a platform for speaking the unspeakable. Before *Emily the Strange* appeared, Constance repeatedly said that staying with the corpse was unbearable. She remembered abruptly stopping the Focusing session with Edwin in 2015 because she really couldn't stand it anymore. In fact, that was exactly her psychological condition at that time.

I remembered that the first time she told me about her depression was one midnight when she was on the verge of breaking down, yelling, "I can't stand it any longer! I am going to collapse." Before that I didn't know she had depression. She hid it very well. Her frank disclosure of her illness happened only a few months before she visualized the corpse in her first Focusing session with Edwin.

Here I recalled the insight of "re-experiencing", initiated by Ikemi Akira, a veteran Focusing mentor and professor in humanistic psychology. By re-experiencing the imageries emerged from Focusing, implicit resources will be fleshed out, encouraging the formation of new narratives. According to Akira, this is not merely the representation of previous experiences, but fresh narratives in the making in the here and now.

In the past week, almost seven years after the corpse's first appearance, Constance could still feel its power. She was very uncomfortable talking about the scene, nervous and evasive. But when Emily the cartoon character came on stage, the tone changed. Constance was able, through Emily, to speak freely, finding that the corpse was no longer in control and she was free to stay or leave. The sudden appearance of Emily was not that mystical, because Constance has been fond of that cartoon character and remains so to this day, but the amazing aspect of her Focusing is that Emily was retrieved from Constance's memory at the perfect time to deal with the situation, giving her a voice to speak out and break free.

In Constance's cleansing ritual with the wool ball, Mrs. Marche, our landlady in Southampton, performed the same magic. Constance remembers that she was always smiling. In the ritual, Mrs. Marche was caring, wearing her smile, meticulously cleaning the knitted doll. Constance was in her loving care. Imagination it was, but the images were filled with the real life remembrance of this lovely lady. It is not too much of a surprise that Constance thought of Mrs. Marche; the magic is that she was able to bring a past memory to the present, and with such precision, to provide the ritual with the loving care most needed to cleanse and to transform.

Edwin pointed out that my companionship was significant in facilitating Constance's imaginative Focusing. I hadn't been aware of that before. Given the trust between us, she felt safe and was ready to open to her meditative exploration. When I look back, I see I was consciously telling her that I was riding beside her. I was actively imagining, vicariously riding, with the wish that she would feel protected along the journey. I guess my companionship was a gentle support that allowed her to bring the imageries forward.

Liz, Cliff, Edwin and I all thought that the simple verse "been here" (到此一遊) was an amazing insight flashing out at the most appropriate moment. It created a capacious psychological space for Constance, enabling her to keep a distance from the corpse. She had been drowned in horror when her arm was caught by the corpse's gripping hand. "Been here" was the profound wisdom of not getting stuck in that. She was free to go.

Liz highlighted the single Chinese character 遊, which means "visit, travel, move around freely", like a fish in the water (the word resembles another Chinese character *swim*). And it is really good advice for those who are trapped in a bad relationship, a depressive state or trauma. You have been there. You know how miserable it was. You have endured, sunk into the abyss. You remember - no repression and avoidance. You move on with your life. The mystical part is why Constance could fish out this "been here" motto. In her mind this dated verse was old-fashioned, but it became the witty and conclusive statement for her imaginative Focusing.

Cliff was mindful throughout the Zoom meeting. He said all the dramatic visualizations that I retold were outward looking, but when Emily appeared, Constance was on stage. It was her agency, her subjectivity, her command of the whole situation. Her inner strength could be seen, and she was clearly in the driver's seat. With his years of Focusing practice, Cliff has learned that when dealing with some thorny problem where all available solutions come to a dead end, where he can't find a cure, that is the time when he has to surrender. More often than not, there comes some advice, a suggestion, a pointer from the felt sense of the body, or from the source of all things, God, if you will. There is a new character, a new name, a new suit, inviting you to put it on and survive. When we are receptive and willing to take up this invitation, there will be a shift, and you will see life with new eyes. That was how Cliff felt when Emily came up to give Constance agency to speak differently.

As I listened to Cliff's sharing, I recalled the moment when Constance said, in a sarcastic tone, "The dumb corpse doesn't have a clue how to deal with me!" She had a "shift" when she talked like Emily. At that moment, I felt as if the teenage Constance was speaking, she was cheerful and witty, free from her psychological bondage.

Chapter 8

The Entanglement of Time and Space

Entangled Timelines, an Unfolding Poem

I started writing this book in April 2022, after the sublime moment at the camphor tree. Since then, I have been following two timelines. The first, beginning on March 23, 2021, documents the dreams and happenings from before the senior staff were first officially held responsible. On the second timeline, I have written my experiences of the day freshly, like writing my diary.

The first timeline follows how this all started and leads to the text message of the Stephen King poem my daughter sent me, which triggered a sea change in subsequent events. The wording of the poem, ever since, has been entwined in my spiritual journey and my daughter's recovery. When I looked back, I could see that these threads were woven together in meaningful coincidences, but I was not sure how to bring these threads together in words. The paragraphs appear in the first few pages of chapter one. In the draft, there was a missing paragraph on synchronicity.

On the second timeline, on September 1, 2022, at around 5:30 pm, I finished writing up what had happened on March 23, 2021. I took a break and picked up my phone. There was a missed call at 5:29 pm, from Wincey, Mr. T's secretary, the man who is handling my case. She had never called me before. The last text I received from her was five months ago when I asked if it was safe for me to leave the city. This was the first time she had called me directly. I smelled something strange. Anxiety burned through my chest, a familiar sensation since last November whenever there is an alert. I called back, no one answered. I guessed they might be in an important meeting with all their mobile phones sealed in a box. My mind started to race. Speculations shot up in the air. It must be important.

I felt intimidated by the sudden upsurge of my own emotions, involuntary reactions out of my control prompted simply by a missed call. All the calmness in meditation that I had experienced in the past few months didn't help a bit. I thought I had conquered fear. I had not.

It was just a call, I sighed, disappointed. How would I react if I were facing a stronger stressor? It would be much worse. I had an urge to call again, to find out what was going on, to ease my anxiety. But calling her frenetically would do no good. There was a record of my missed call on her phone already, she would call back if it was urgent. Waiting was quite a fretful torture.

I took some deep breaths and tried to calm myself. I didn't struggle with wild speculations of "what if this" and "what if that". I looked up the paragraphs I had just written an hour earlier and found the poem in my notepad again:

"We did not ask for this room or this music. We were invited in. Therefore, because the dark surrounds us, let us turn our faces to the light. Let us endure hardship to be grateful for plenty.

We have been given pain to be astounded by joy. We have been given life to deny death.

We did not ask for this room or this music. But because we are here, let us dance."

I felt the gravity of darkness in the panic I was in, but I gradually turned my face to the light. I stepped back to give myself some inner space, let the anxiety come through, and pass on. Hardship and pain are heavy, they take a toll on the body. I felt the weight, but, in facing the light, the heaviness was gradually released. It was not easy, but after maybe half an hour I was calm again. I had found my peace. The urge to call and to know what was happening had softened.

I drove Constance home from work and cooked dinner for the family. Usually we walk together after dinner, and I will wait if she has some work to do. But, wanting to spend some time alone, I went on my own and mindfully walked along the waterfront, going over what had happened two hours ago.

Once again, I let the ebb and flow pass on the surface and rested on the inner peace deep inside my heart. I reminded myself to live moment by moment, and I found peace by just enjoying the graceful-looking trees on the sidewalk and the stars in the far sky.

Then to my surprise, I bumped into Barbie, the long haired English sheepdog well-known in the neighborhood. For more than two years we'd met him (yes, a he – with a girlish name like Barbie) almost every evening during our after-dinner walk, but we'd not seen him for months. We thought he might be sick or perhaps had even died. According to the Filipino maid who walked him every day, he was 13 years old – very old for large dogs like him.

To me, and especially to Constance, Barbie was a special friend. He greeted us enthusiastically every time we met, wearing a broad smile, body wriggling, tail wagging, circling between our legs. He was happy all the time. He had a soft and cheerful temperament distinct from all other neighborhood dogs. When Constance was in distress and we were Focusing together, picturing Barbie in her mind became a source of calming energy. For us, "the Barbie attitude" has been a motto. We even have a Chinese calligraphy of his name on our door, to remind us to be cheerful and smiling in difficult times.

I was surprised and elated to see him strolling along the waterfront again, this time with his owner, a lady in her 60s. I guessed the routine of walking Barbie had been changed. That was a happy coincidence. I didn't make the connection at that point, that, walking mindfully, I was exactly having the Barbie attitude in my unexpected reunion with the dog. I took a picture of him and sent it to Constance. She called back, shouting, "Why wasn't it me who bumped into him?"

She joined me after she was done with her work. We had a nice, long discussion about the obscure poem she sent me, which she reads over and over. Had I not scrolled back to the text messages sent a year ago, the poem would have slipped from my mind. Apparently, it was recited at the end of a mini-series adapted from one of Stephen King's lesser-known novels: the story of a time-traveler who meets his once-in-a-lifetime lover in the past. Back in his present time his lover is already 80 years old. He is invited to her retirement party, and the episode ends when the dancing music fades in and their eyes meet. The poem, which was not in the novel, was recited when everything had come to a close. Stephen King, in his 70s, wrote the poem specially for the mini-series. On the surface, the poem is about the nostalgia of unrealizable love, age differences irreconcilable, time irreversible. But the poem transcends romantic love. It speaks to those caught in uninvited circumstances, burdened by hardship and pain. It also carries the spiritual message of surrendering to the situation and dancing with it, turning to the light, enduring hardship, defying death, being grateful, and being astounded by the joy of our very existence.

When Constance first heard the poem, she was touched and cried her eyes out. Echoing the verses, she felt trapped in her depression, surrounded by darkness, confined with no escape. She felt the pain, but the light was beyond reach. I remembered sharing with her the Gospel of St John verse 1:5, of light shining into, and effortlessly extinguishing the darkness. But she felt, at that time, that light was painful, that she couldn't step into the light. Now she has gradually reached out and has had a taste of the unconditional love of this all-embracing light.

Recalling the challenges of our family, I have a better grasp of the non-duality depicted in the poem, of light and darkness, pain and joy, hardship and gratitude, life and death. The two sides are seemingly contradictory, but together they harmonize the mystery of life. Ignoring the dark side, and pushing "positive thinking" can be oppressive and toxic. Indulging ourselves inside the shell of our miseries, all we may see is darkness.

When darkness is all around, turning our face toward the light is so precious a gift for we earthly souls; joy and gratitude are such a consolation amid pain and suffering. The poem speaks of our vulnerability, compassion and resilience, the sacred stones at the high temple of our humanity.

Constance reminded me that the tattoo on her arm, the image of a hand reaching for a star, was a design based on this poem. She had taken it with her as an idea for the artist. I had almost forgotten this part of the story. Now I see how significant this poem has been to her. She carries it permanently on her arm. And the poem has become meaningful to me too after that eventful evening in 2021.

The Unfolding Synchronicity

I woke in the early hours of the morning. My mind was clear, recalling the full sequence of the synchronicity I had gone through:

- Six years ago my daughter watched the mini-series 11.22.63 and was deeply touched by the poem *Facing the Light* which was recited at the end.
- March 23, 2021. Parked by the roadside, and in a peculiar situation, I received a call at midnight and wrote my column on an empty basketball court as I waited for my distressed daughter to get off from work. I encouraged her by citing the poem she had shared with me some years earlier. That night was the starting point of my strange spiritual journey.
- September 1, 2022. I wrote about that night in March 2021, recalling the already-forgotten poem. I sensed some strange coincidences in how it all started. I wrote what had happened but was not sure how to close off the ending. I made a wish for some inspiration and waited with anticipation.

- I finished writing, leaving out the last paragraph on synchronicity. The secretary called right after that, but I missed the call. I was anxious. The anxiety escalated when she didn't return my call. The poem calmed me down.
- After dinner, walking alone, I experienced the joy and gratitude described in the poem, and I bumped into Barbie the cheerful dog, who hadn't been seen for months.
- My daughter joined me and we had a long discussion about the poem, which left an imprint on her road to recovery, and unexpectedly intertwined with my spiritual journey. The poem was symbolized and carried permanently on Constance's arm.
- In the afternoon, I discovered that the secretary's missed call was just a misdial, insignificant, but meaningful to me when placed in the context of these unrelated coincidences.
- At the beginning, I wanted to quote some generalizations on coincidence that the psychiatrist Bernard Beitman has made in his book *Connecting with Coincidence*. But I was not satisfied with copying and pasting a summary of his book to mine. So, I waited, asking for fresh experiences to illustrate Beitman's framework.
- Right after writing about receiving the telephone call in 2021, I received the mistaken call from Wincey. I got what I asked for, and much richer than I might have expected.

Here is the summary, citing Beitman, together with my synchronistic experiences. Generalizing from hundreds of testimonies, Beitman states that there are four factors that increase the likelihood of coincidences happening: high emotion, transition, seeking, and altered routines. My case is on the mark for three of these.

- High emotion: I was waiting for my distressed daughter and sharing her agonies (March 23, 2021); and I was on high alert when I missed a call from my lawyer (September 1, 2022).
- Seeking: I was looking for ways to comfort my daughter (I got the poem); and I was anticipating something happening so that I could write on synchronicity with something substantial (I got the missed call and a full story to write about).
- Altered routine: I waited for my daughter on the street for 6 hours (and received a call that changed course for our family); I didn't wait for my daughter as I usually did. I walked on my own and bumped into Barbie (his cheerfulness echoing my state of mind at that moment).

I was not exactly in the middle of a life transition as Beitman has tabled, but as coincidences have been unfolding, I was diligently experimenting with my new-found spirituality.

According to my background in ethnographic research, my experiences of synchronicity, as recorded in various parts of this book, tell me time and again that there is an in-between space between me and other beings (especially the people I love dearly), between all the existential conditions we are in, and between us and Mother Nature. The connections are, as yet, beyond our comprehension. I'm open to what this in-between space has to offer and have become more sensitive to the inspirations given to me when I walk into coincidences like the ones I have just written about.

What are the implications for my course of action and my future? I am pretty sure of my spiritual pursuit: to go deeper into my inner peace, practice more, and prepare for the challenges given to me and my family. I still have a long way to go; the in-between space is an intriguing dimension for me to explore.

"Coincidences are not exotic flowers growing only under special circumstances. They are more like common wildflowers popping up all around us." – Bernard Beitman.

The Premonition of the Three-headed Dragon

As my two timelines intertwine, the coincidences multiply.

A few days ago, I wrote about a dream I had two years ago (page 15, chapter one). It was the first time I had dreamt of a mythic figure, a three-headed dragon writhing on a rocky shore. At the time, I was anxious to probe whether the dragon had something to do with Jung's archetypal symbols, so I asked my friends for their input, but my friends had nothing to say about the dragon. It was not on their radar at all.

I wrote about that dream in Chinese. Two years later, while translating the essay into English for this book, the anxiety aroused by the dragon in that dream came alive for me again. I found it quite similar to what I felt whenever I was triggered by news associated with my case. I told myself it was quite normal for deep-seated fears to emerge in my dream in the form of a fierce and malicious dragon. It was an understandable expression of my anxiety buried deep in my unconscious.

Out of curiosity, I flipped through my dream diary and found that the dream was from January 29, 2021, two months *before* I was invited to the initiative. I always thought it had happened afterward. Given that, the dragon was not so easy to explain away as unprocessed anxiety; at the time of dreaming I was not involved in any legal danger. It suddenly dawned on me that the three-headed dragon might well be, like the hunch I had early on, an instance of Jung's archetypal symbol, a mythic figure from the collective, piercing through the boundary of the personal. It might even be a precognition of my involvement in the case before it all started.

In ancient mythology, dragons appear in a wide variety of legends, bringing contradictory meanings of destruction and good fortune. Myths of a three-headed dragon, sometimes as a three-headed dog, are less diversified, mostly indicating a fear-invoking monster serving as the watchdog of hidden treasures. My dreaming of the three-headed dragon before my entanglement with financial dispute is comparable to Constance's dreaming of a grass frog (a symbol of fertility) before the miraculous return of her menstruation (page 63). My sense of awe is the same. My dragon dream was incomprehensible to me at the time, but after two years it makes good sense as an object of fear and apprehension. The mythic symbol got into my dream and crisscrossed a sequence of significant events in my life. The symbol didn't cause any physical event to happen. The psychological and the physical do not have a cause-and-effect relationship, but the coincidences are meaningful to me personally. In the dream, I traveled with a group of people in a small boat. When I got to the shore I bumped into a three-headed dragon. It was threatening, but I was able to walk past it and enter the train station. The lesson I learned from the dream workshop last year was to follow the advice of the station master in the dream: to walk backward as a way forward, to focus not only on finding the way home, but to be mindful of the present moment, and be a caring companion to my fellow citizens.

The dream has been unfolding in my daily life, going through my ordeal, facing the dragon, learning the lessons, and being a good companion to those in the same boat on a rough sea. Incidentally, on an ordinary day recently, triggered by a trivial news image on a train, I experienced a sudden upsurge of anxiety. However, I've begun to learn how to face my fear squarely, let go of my anger and resentment. Whether in real life I could walk out of the danger as I did in the dream is beyond my knowing, but I am grateful that the dream reveals to me a new mythic meaning. It is another synchronicity for my spiritual growth, which transcends suffering and opens the door to forgiveness, compassion and companionship.

We dream, but most of our dreams are forgotten. Trivialities of the day become random imageries of the night. Little dreams come and go, maintaining the rhythm of our biological clock and psychological balance. They don't make much sense and beg no serious deliberation. But when we arrive at a particular juncture of our life, when our society is facing colossal changes, big dreams flourish, full of energies. As if they are hidden letters yet to be opened, invitations yet to be accepted, they reach out to us from the deep sea of the unconscious and provide us with courage for a breakthrough into uncharted lands. A Jungian bent if you may, these big dreams are an articulation of ancient myths for contemporary souls.

I keep a dream journal, and over the course of a few years, I have come to an understanding that, despite most dream contents arising from life experiences and imaginative projection, there are quite a few images and imageries beyond my personal history and imagination. They emerge from deep inside me, but they seem to originate from times and places far beyond my comprehension. I believe the symbol of the three-headed dragon is one of these ancient mythic figures that made its way into the trajectories of my life and the city.

A Precognition Too Good to Be True

K-Town was hit by a typhoon in early September 2022. The day after the storm, the sky cleared up as Constance and I walked along the waterfront. Constance had a dream on that stormy night. It was in black and white. She thought the dream was about a discontented city, hit hard by the pandemic and the following social downturn. "People are rejoicing. What a relief if it is true!" She stared at the dark sky, with faint hope and serious doubt in her eyes.

In her dream, the city, engulfed by dark mists, was permeated with a sense of dread. She retold her dream in the present tense.

"This world has no color. On the streets, people roam without purpose, dragging their feet as they pace. A hollow whistle comes from up above the sky, a big feisty genie takes a deep breath and claps his hands. A loud bomb, a gust of strong wind, the mists and clouds gather and swirl like they are trapped inside a cotton candy machine. Then everything swoops off, dark mists gone, together with the lifelessness and dreadfulness of the city, blown away, followed by a sigh of relief from the big fat giant. The sky is clear. I have a panoramic view of the streets and buildings, the open sea, and the mountain ridges in the distant background. People are rejoicing."

Towards the end of the dream, Constance was aware of its strange optimism. While still asleep she exclaimed, "No, this is too good to be true, it must be wishful thinking!" She was lucid dreaming, aware that she was having a strange dream while still in her dream.

She was puzzled about the nature of this dream as the images and feelings were so distinctive. Most of her other dreams were personal and private, but this one brought feelings that were kind of collective. In the dream, she first felt dreadful and later rejoiced together with the crowd. Adding to her puzzlement was the fact that for the past few years she has been, and still is, quite detached from local affairs. She doesn't read local news and is totally apathetic about turbulent public sentiments. On the contrary, her emotional attachment is to the news abroad. She would take a day off work just to follow the major elections in the UK and the United States. Her psychiatrist said this might well be a defense mechanism for her, designed to fend off distress. She already has too much personal stress to deal with. This black-and-white dream was a rare occasion on which she could share the emotions of her fellow citizens.

At the back of our minds we both suspected it was a precognition dream, but we had serious reservations. We didn't want to give this too-good-to-be-true fantasy the slightest chance to shine. Not that we didn't want to see rainbows – quite the opposite. It is a secret wish deep in our hearts; but a rosy dream like this one was too naïve, simple-minded and gullible; the genie imagery was too cartoonish and childish for us to give it serious thought. But I guess there's no harm in writing it down, just for the record.

Maybe I was swayed by Constance's dream, because my meditation the day after manifested similar imagery. About half an hour into my relaxed state, I was calm, feeling like a branch connected to the generously giving vine. Gently coming forth were the many difficult as well as blissful moments of my life, one by one, carrying emotions with them for me to re-experience. And the scene swiftly changed.

I was enjoying a clear view of the purplish sky against Tiger Ridge, a landmark symbolizing the vibrant city at its best. The rocky ridge resembles the shape of a crouching tiger, sitting magnificently in the radiant lights of the setting sun. In my vision people were rejoicing under Tiger Ridge at the Mid-Autumn Festival.

The above was written on a day in the fall of 2022. It is a record of our dream and vision, held deep in our hearts.

The Tiger Ridge Vision in an Exhibition

On September 10, 2022, the people of K-Town celebrated the Chinese Mid-Autumn Festival – the day of the brightest and biggest full moon of the whole year. The Lunar Calendar doesn't correspond to the New Calendar, so each year this Chinese Mid-Autumn Festival falls on a different New Calendar date. Constance celebrated with her boyfriend Fred and his family, while Teresa and I dined out and took a walk along the waterfront after dinner. The mega-size moon was hanging low at the far end of the sky. Kids were toying with lanterns and candles. The festive mood reminded me of my vision the week before, where K-Town citizens were rejoicing at the Mid-Autumn Festival.

A day before the festival, Kenny invited me to a photo exhibition entitled *Views of the Tiger* by the French photographer

R. Jac, who came to K-Town in 2009 and has lived here ever since. I have known Kenny for many years, and this was the first time he had invited me to join him for an outing. We visited the gallery in the afternoon of the exhibition's first day. A particular photo of the Tiger Ridge resonated deeply within me. I was moved. It was as if I could feel the heart of the tiger, caring so much about the city. It took some time for me to recognize that the feeling was what I had felt in my meditation.

As we enjoyed the festive mood along the waterfront, the image of the Tiger Ridge came up again, and I felt the urge to share this story of meaningful coincidence. I told Teresa about Constance's dream and the similar imagery I had seen in my meditation, and the connection with the photo I saw in the exhibition. The ridge, in all its ruggedness, was tender at heart. In the photo, the head of the tiger was so close to a compact building that one could feel the companionship between the mythical ridge and the ordinary people of K-Town. I told Teresa that this was the reason why I had bought the photo-book of the exhibition to take home.

Teresa has a rational and analytic mind, usually not that receptive to my spiritual experiences. I appreciate her skepticism, which for me has been a check and balance for a more evidence-based judgment of the journey our family has undergone. Interestingly, this time she did not play the role of adversary; instead she pointed out an interesting observation that I had missed, namely that all of Constance's other dreams have been gloomy, hectic, violent, and dark. This was the only one with a cheerful ending, so out of character that the dream seemed to be not from her usual self.

When we came back home, I was eager to read the photo-book of the exhibition. I turned the pages for the first time and had a strong feeling of synchronicity. The felt sense in my meditation was beyond the mastery of words. But, flipping through the book, the photos resonated with my feelings, not conveyed by words, but by the sharp edges of rocks, the steep lines of buildings, and the intimate lighting of the twilight and magic hours. I could feel the throbbing heart of an outsider-turned-native photographer. He followed his girlfriend to her home city of K-Town twelve years ago and was captivated by the Tiger Ridge the moment he arrived. He regularly visited his in-laws for birthday dinners and traditional celebrations. Many of those gatherings took place near Tiger Ridge and he recalls in the afterword of his book, that always in his mind is the imposing vision of the crouching tiger atop the mountain, quietly watching over the city. Coincidentally, that was exactly the feeling in my mind, of an empathic tiger dutifully watching over the city in difficult times.

As coincidences flood into my life more frequently, they seem to have evolved and become more and more intricate. The vision began with Constance's unusual dream, followed by my vision, then the exhibition, the timing of the Mid-Autumn Festival, and the photographer's personal encounter with the Tiger Ridge. They were linked not by causality, but by the meaning-making process of my "subjective" felt sense.

***

(A year later, a few days before the Mid-Autumn Festival of 2023, when the first draft of the book had been written, I hiked on the Chevy's Ride with a group of friends. While walking on a winding trail, I remembered this Tiger Ridge vision of last year. As I was struggling with the fact of the vision and its improbability, a striking panoramic view appeared before my eyes. The sky was clear, white clouds were high and gigantic, the mountain ridges were majestic. I had a hunch that this was what Constance had seen in her dream. Strangely, she hadn't seen Tiger Ridge in her dream, but in front of me, right in the middle of the ridges, was the tiny but clear profile of the Tiger

Ridge. I took a photo, sent it to Constance, and asked whether this was what she had seen in her dream a year ago. She said yes. Tiger Ridge, blended in the panorama, had been in her dream without her knowing it. K-Town is still undergoing drastic social changes and people are pessimistic. Constance's dream and my vision paint a different future in which people are rejoicing. We hope they will come true.

Chapter 9

The Magic Garden and Lessons for Daily Awakening

The Magic Garden

I had always wanted to bring Constance to Karrie Garden to see whether she could connect with the giant trees. The last time I was there, some of her nightmarish blockages were disentangled in unexpected ways. I wondered what it would be like if she could stand in front of the trees herself.

She finally made time to pay a visit. To many, sensing the energy of trees is a delicate, perhaps other-worldly idea. It is vivid for some but nonsensical for others. When we strolled along the trails, I kept an open mind letting Constance freely explore the woods. We visited the "energy gate" (two Sweetgum trees paired side by side to resemble a gateway), the mother tree (a big camphor tree in a deep valley), and the father tree (another, bigger camphor tree at the end of the trail).

We spent half a day in the garden. Constance didn't say much about her experiences with the trees and I didn't ask. It was a relaxing trip, sufficient to enjoy the green and the sun.

It wasn't until after dinner, as we walked along the waterfront, that she started sharing her encounters with the trees. There had been some concrete "dialogue" between them, but Constance was hesitant, and she began with a skeptical question: *Was I imagining all this?* ... However, she was enthusiastically engaged. The sensation she got from the trees was as if they were taking deep breaths, slow and steady. The interactions between them were as if they were talking to each other.

Her first conversation was with the two Sweetgum trees at the "energy gate," as PH, the Karrie tutor called it. Constance said they were like a pair of twins, witty and energetic. She shared with them her insatiable desire to conquer and get recognition, and her endless search for meanings. The twins told her that she didn't have to go anywhere, that life came back full circle.

After lunch, I took Constance to the mother tree. Last time, most of us in the group had felt her generosity. I told Constance this would be the ONE for her on this trip, and I invited her to spend some time alone in the area. Nothing happened there, she later told me.

She strolled around and was drawn to another tree, a grandmother tree, which greeted her directly, saying, "My child, all is fine." The tree was like a granny, cheerful and caring. Constance told granny about her conversation with the twins and asked what the twins meant by "not having to go anywhere." She became cheerful when she talked about the granny tree, she jokingly mimicked the theatrical voice, "Reach out..., reach out for the sun. Life. Alive." The encounter was warmhearted, but Constance didn't know what it meant to reach for the sun.

It took some twists for us to find the biggest camphor tree that I had visited last time but it was worth the trouble. Constance told me that the tree was like a grandfather, with a firm hold on his ground. He was not as approachable as the granny tree, and his answer was succinct. Constance asked what the meaning of "reach for the sun" was. The grandpa tree answered, "You are a special child. Look inside. You have a reservoir there, and your roots are deep. Lot of things for you to discover."

Constance's Account

I was paraphrasing Constance's conversation with the trees. Why not ask her to tell her account directly? So, she did, as follows:

Half skeptical, half excited, I was introduced to the twinned Sweetgums by the gate to a garden. I stood between their magnetic fields. They gave me a jolly greeting. Strained as to how I should approach them, I laid bare my insecurities in the hope of receiving some counsel.

"My desires are insatiable, I wish to be recognized, to be loved and to conquer by every means possible..." Somehow, they had drawn out an unusual degree of naked candor in our first encounter. Two teardrops made their way down my face, quietly.

"Where?" they asked.

"I am constantly looking for the right path." I murmured.

Standing between them, it continually felt like when I was looking at one, the other would give me a nudge, like a pair of mischievous boys. Unrelenting chatter.

"Why?" A brief pause. "You'd always come full circle."

I fixed my gaze on them for a moment. Nodded, expressed my thanks and said goodbye. Essentially they are telling me, "Stop looking for what you are looking for."

We took the minivan uphill, passed my new acquaintances, the Sweetgums, and stopped at the Fern Walk. After a brief climb, I sat by the mother. There are four to five ferns nestled on this towering camphor in the mid-levels, intertwined with climbing plants and surrounded by ferns and saplings. Shimmering sunlight and steady frequencies, but nothing more.

"Hello, I was told you are the mother."

Silence. The evergreen vines breathed with her, but I could not manage to interrupt nor get any response. Not prepared to give up, especially with the mother, I sat, I waited, I opened up my senses, to no avail.

In concert, I felt a thumping pulse. It led me to this mountainous camphor by the roadside, lodged in the river streams, a trench by the slope.

"Hello ma'am."

"All. Is. Well, my child," roaring with a laugh, a deep, rumbling and gentle sound. She has plenty of draping vines, making her look like an Indian granny, like Coco (in the animated film). I rested my palm on her trunk, and she chuckled again.

"I am lost."

"Life. Energy. Appears in all forms. Everything always comes back to life. Always. Even for the dead, even in the dead." She spoke resoundingly, "You look for energy."

"Where, may I ask?"

"Reach for the sun," she bellowed, but gently in a heartening way.

"Moon?" I asked.

"The Sun. Reach for the sun. REACH." Followed by her now signature chuckles. "Reach!"

I said my farewell and moved on.

Dad had said there's a "Tree Supreme" we should look out for. Eventually, down by the pond, the hulk came before our eyes. He firmly rests down in the earth with his mighty torso. There is an absence of climbing leaves, instead he has stiff thick bark all over him, with branches stretching far out to the sky. Flickering beams of light hunker down between leaves lashing about. The drumming beats were echoing ever more, stroking down my core. The papa tree was solemn.

"Granny says, I should reach for the sun." I mouthed the words.

"You are special, my child. Reach in. Reach inside." He reached out at the same time, cradling my heart. "There is a reservoir here. Spend your life reaching inside."

He was somber. I froze. He reminded me of my loving grandpa though, offering tender warmth. I thanked him, and turned my focus to the glaring rays of the sun by the stone walls of the valley.

The Language of Nature

Constance's encounter with the trees is mysterious, it seems to me. In fact, taken at face value, the wisdom given by the trees for Constance is dense and needs further pondering. The nature of communication is worthy of some conscientious deliberation.

So, we had a long session of Focusing on the three conversations she had had with the trees. It was a mindful exercise to sense each small component of her experiences.

The first encounter was at the "energy gate." She was alone there, a bit disoriented, as she was new to this. But once she felt the energy field, she naturally opened up to the two gum trees. "I said I wished to be loved. I have never used the word *love* so directly to express my inner need. Nor would I choose to say *conquer*. It is too strong a word. But what I said at that moment was genuine. Normally, I filter my true feelings. In front of the twins, I didn't have to." Constance said she was in tears because she was touched by her own naked miseries, and the receptive understanding of the two gum trees.

"They are non-judgmental…" I said to her, remembering the notes given to us by Clara, our French tree teacher.

Constance's response was quick. "The word non-judgmental doesn't feel right. That is advice for us humans who are judgmental. Trees simply don't judge. They are benign." She is right and on point; trees don't judge at all from the start.

She talked about the chattering between the two gum trees, but when I asked her to focus on the experiential nature of that chattering, she said it was like energy, or frequencies, bouncing back and forth. Constance is super sensitive to words and visuals, which is why she used the word chattering to describe her experience of the energy bouncing, which was like what I felt at the "energy gate". When I walked past the gate, I felt as if two magnets were interacting with each other and I was caught in the middle.

As Constance focused on the sensation of the moment, she "heard" the message "Come full circle." She recalled the feeling of "withering", as if an engine at full throttle suddenly ran out of steam. She felt lost. If all her efforts in adult life came full circle, what else could she be looking for?

I know Constance well. She has been striving so hard to find a meaningful way of life. The sudden Zen insight into her futile striving was like a bowl of cold water spilled upon a hot stove. But according to my own experience, the diminishing of the ego makes perfect sense on the path of spiritual enlightenment, and I think spending less time *doing* and more time *being* is a good intervention for her hectic life. Her sense of "withering" is in fact a chance for her to look beyond her high achieving ego.

Before visiting Karrie Garden, I talked about the mother tree a lot. Constance had imagined a lot about the tree and expected something to happen there. If her conversation with the trees came from her imagination, the mother tree was a good object for projection and transference. She was disappointed. I guess active imagination on her part alone just can't actualize an interaction. There must be some actual experiential exchange between Constance and the trees to achieve a comprehensible encounter.

The mother tree was not that responsive to Constance. But in contrast, the granny tree, just a few meters away, was chatty and welcoming. She felt the tree was fond of having her around. When we did some Focusing to re-experience the interaction, she discerned some minute differences: the granny tree and the nearby ferns and shrubs shared an energy field among themselves, but when granny "communicated" with her, it was in a different mode, with messages short and brief, as if granny was speaking in a second language. With a closer look, what she received from granny was not exactly "conversational English", but comprehensible sensations that Constance could put into words. The key message was life and energy. "When granny said *reach for the sun*, there was actually an uplifting energy and a posture of stretching out towards the sky and reaching for the energy from above."

I paid full attention as I listened to Constance's recalling of her experience. It resonated inside me that the "language" of granny and the content of what she was "saying" were congruent with the habitat: the cycle of life, the flourishing valley, the running stream, and the generous sun. It is the language of nature, not of Constance the city girl.

The last conversation was with the grandpa tree, which had a very different vibe. The tree was firm and somewhat detached, like a wise man. Constance said she was frozen, as if her legs were rooted to the ground. That was my sensation too, with the giant camphor tree at Tate Basin: a solid sensation of grounding, energy rising from the soil. Granny asked Constance to reach out, but grandpa asked her to look inside. This makes sense to me too. My spiritual awakening points to a similar experience where the energy outside and my inner being are one.

I asked Constance about the choice of the word "reservoir". "What does it mean when grandpa told you to look at the reservoir inside of you?" She said she in fact had an image of a body of water, the word reservoir was her description of what was in her mind. She understands it in tandem with the twins' saying, "Come in full circle," that she doesn't have to look elsewhere for treasures, there is a reservoir within.

This was a very fruitful Focusing experience for both of us. I am quite certain that the encounters were based on substantial exchanges, not simply from Constance's own imagination, because the contents were firmly situated in the natural habitat, and not from her everyday life. She is not familiar with, and oftentimes resistant to, the language of spirituality, but at Karrie she was quite at home with it. There are different forms of energy and ways of communication between Nature and humans: visual, auditory, via sensations, or otherwise discernible for the initiated. Different people have different degrees and range of sensitivity towards other life forms. Constance's conversation with trees is in fact non-verbal. She is very sensitive and intuitive in using words as "containers" to hold the "messages" she received from the trees. The wisdom she got from Karrie is relevant to the life situation she is currently in: stop chasing, reach for the source of life, and be sensitive to the resources within. The trees have given us wisdom to live our lives. They are generous. We are both grateful.

Seeking to Understand

In his book *The Direct Way,* Adyashanti integrates spiritual insight into daily life. His persistent view is that spiritual growth is a continual process of becoming, an embodiment of awakening in our lifelong human expression. Awakening shouldn't be taken as a spiritual accomplishment to be put in our pocket as a prize. In recent weeks, I have been following the exercises in Adyashanti's book to bring my spiritual insights into daily practice.

"Seek to understand before seeking to be understood." This is a familiar verse from a hymn I used to sing in church when I was young. It was almost 40 years ago. I still remember the hymn very well; it is a prayer attributed to Saint Francis. Adyashanti turns this hymn into a practice which is having a transformative effect on me. He addresses directly to something I was unaware of myself:

"We all love being understood. In one way or another, we're often seeking this—but if you're not careful, that wonderful experience of being understood, as healing and affirming as it can be, may develop into a subtle or sometimes overt demand. Even if we're not speaking in a demanding or insistent way, we can approach interactions in a manner that demands we are understood before we understand."

Indeed, I have a strong desire to let my friends know what has happened to me, how much I have suffered, and how heavy the burden has been on me. But throughout, I have had to keep silent to avoid arousing unnecessary fears among them, so only a few know about my situation. Since I am on the fringe of the incident, I have never been targeted by critics in the media and was only named once or twice at the margin of news stories, so, my predicament was largely unseen. Sometimes when I met with friends I had an urge to tell my story, a hidden story that demanded to be heard; but of course I suppressed this urge and kept my mouth shut.

After reading Adyashanti, I became aware of my desire to be understood. It had been there whenever I was in a small gathering with friends. I was keen to look for a window to tell my story, unaware of the subtle impetus behind my urge. I followed the steps of Focusing and paid attention to the bodily sensation of that urge, and let my hidden emotions unfold. There were a lot of things going on. My egoic way of thinking was that such a drama had happened in my life, therefore my friends should recognize my sufferings and give me some credit for enduring it all. My rational mind prohibited me from making such a self-centered and childish demand on others, thus the nature of that urge was out of my sight and my awareness. There was bitterness and grievance too, the unfortunate nature of my ordeal, my enduring the threat while others were enjoying life as usual. To complicate matters, there was a spiritual ego, benign on the surface, subtly arrogant at the core, framing the drama as special and unique, and me as a sage, worthy of praise.

When I became aware of these intrigues, it was relatively easy for me to let go. As Adyashanti has written:

"The most important person to understand you is you, because nobody is ever going to understand you in the way that you understand yourself. The funny thing that happens when you deeply understand yourself is the demand that others understand you begins to disappear. It's nice when that melts away, because your heart opens, your mind opens, and life is more enjoyable."

There is a deep sense of relief. In fact, with all the meaningful coincidences, inspiring dreams, reassuring moments in my meditative and Focusing practices that I have gone through, I have been healed. Suffering has turned into spiritual growth, self-awareness, and better family relationships. The urge to tell my story was in fact another blockage. Once it had surfaced, it melted away.

In a recent gathering I put into practice Adyashanti's exercise to listen with empathy and to be sensitive to my desire to be understood. I was with a few of my former research partners, who seemed to have guessed that I was involved in some difficult situation, although I hadn't disclosed any details to them at all. Before the meeting, I prepared myself to have a heart open to listen, to know more, to care about my friends. I wished to be a good listener instead of a self-perceived victim ventilating my grievance.

We gathered at my friend's cozy home. Interestingly, the urge to tell my "dramatic" story was still there, but it was like a guy with a blushing face, wanting to break out but immediately backing down. There was another part of me comforting this impetuous guy, telling him that I was fine, I was being taken care of, there was no need to cry out for attention. When I opened my heart to listen to the interesting and sometimes painful experiences of my friends I realized that, one way or another, drastic social changes had impacted people from all walks of life; my friends and I were not exempt.

I didn't talk about my story at all, but I found strength and encouragement just by listening to the struggles of others. It was a therapeutic experience for all of us. And for me, the prayer of Saint Francis has a personal impact here in this fellowship of friends.

"O Divine Master,

Grant that I may not so much seek to be consoled, as to console;

To be understood, as to understand;
To be loved as to love.
For it is in giving that we receive;
It is in pardoning that we are pardoned;
And it is in dying that we are born to eternal life."

Forgive, the Great Lesson of Compassion

The last exercise of Adyashanti's book is forgiveness. The full title is *"releasing yourself from the past through forgiveness"*. With the two-year long pandemic, the loss of loved ones, the breaking up of social ties, mass emigration; there are wounds unhealed, traumas repressed, conflicts unresolved. People are still carrying heavy burdens of resentment, hatred, despair, and deep-seated sadness. There are those whose sufferings are way beyond my imagination. I am not one of those hardest hit, but still, it has been a tough challenge for me. To be honest, it is difficult to let go. Adyashanti writes:

"Forgiveness is about letting go—and these are strong words, but I'll use them anyway—letting go of hatred, rage, and resentment, which are all hindrances on the path to insight. Forgiveness releases you from the clutches of the past. When you forgive someone else, you release yourself from them. When you forgive yourself, you release yourself from the past. You allow yourself to evolve, to grow."

Indeed, releasing myself from the past is what I need. It strikes a chord deep inside. If I am still clinging onto the unresolved wounds of the past, I am in fact denying myself a much more fruitful life at hand. Some of my friends who were devastated by unexpected misfortune told me that their pain and anger keep them going, reminding them not to forget, motivating them to endure. Here, Adyashanti's teaching is helpful:

"There is often confusion about forgiveness, so let me make one thing clear: Forgiveness doesn't mean forgetfulness. It doesn't mean denying a painful experience. Nothing is being denied. Forgiveness is not bypassing something or sweeping it under the carpet. For a lot of people, it's a strange idea that you could not deny something has happened, not deny your own pain, yet simultaneously not hold onto rage and resentment. When we hold onto rage and resentment, it keeps the painful event alive in us. In other words, we're doing painful things to ourselves when we're not letting it go. Letting go sounds easy, but if you feel hurt or wronged or if you have hurt or wronged another, it's not that simple. We must bring the heart into it. It's not an intellectual exercise, it's a heartful exercise."

For me, the most difficult task is to forgive those who inflicted pain on others. I don't want to write explicitly about wrongdoers and wrongdoings, suffice it to say that when these images come to my mind intense emotions would spontaneously be aroused. But I know that carrying resentments is painful and burdensome. I have read Thich Nhat Hanh's poem *Call Me by my True Name* many times. I appreciate the Zen master's compassion towards the pirate who raped and killed. In his memoir, he said he was deeply agonized when he first heard of the news of a young refugee girl being raped, and her father killed, in a boat on the way out of Vietnam. After some difficult inner work, he came to the understanding that the pirates were not conscious of their true nature when they committed those terrible crimes. The poet wrote:

I am the mayfly metamorphosing
on the surface of the river.
And I am the bird
that swoops down to swallow the mayfly.
I am the frog swimming happily
in the clear water of a pond.
And I am the grass-snake
that silently feeds itself on the frog.
...

Please call me by my true names,
so I can hear all my cries and my laughter at once,
so I can see that my joy and pain are one.
Please call me by my true names,
so I can wake up,
and so the door of my heart
can be left open,
the door of compassion.

I could comprehend the latent meaning of this poem, but in my heart there is a big obstacle that prevents me from showing compassion to those who are reckless and cruel. Now, reading the poem one more time, I notice that the space inside me is bigger and can accommodate a bit more.

In my spiritual journey so far, synchronicities have been more frequent. They have strengthened my faith in the possibility of change and in the interconnectedness between the tangible and the unseen, as if there are webs and links, invisible to the naked eye, but lucid for the receptive heart. I have had some first-hand experience of my own changes. I know what it is like to have a self-centered and self-perpetuating ego take over the task of steering my life. For many years, I was not aware of my spiritual self and my ability to love and forgive. At various points I had a death wish for myself because I had already achieved what I had set out to do in life. I poured acid onto the root of a tree that blocked the view of my balcony. I wished for the tree to be uprooted by typhoons so that I could have my nice view back. I had a death wish for my mother too. She was then in her 90s. Dying would be best for her and for others.

These morally forbidden impulses were elusive. They were there, at the back of my mind, but I brushed them aside. These "petty crimes" and "malicious thoughts" of mine are trivial when compared to rape, murder, human rights violations, and war crimes. But I guess the human logic behind petty crime and evil deeds is more or less the same. Humanity is a mixed bag of nobility and brutality. With this awareness, I choose to let go. I gather the courage to forgive my own wrongdoings as well as those of others, but not by forgetting and justifying. Evil and wrong deeds shouldn't be justified by any whitewashing. They must be condemned and rebuked. But I have faith and hope in humanity, just like me. I was blind before, now I see. Earthly beings we are, all having a divine seed in our soul, waiting to be awakened.

[illegible] behind [illegible] and [illegible] must be contaminated and resolved. But I have faith and hope in humanity, that like me, I was blind before now I see clearly

Chapter 10

Meta-Coincidences, Golden Lilies, and the Riddle Dream

As coincidences have accumulated in recent months, they start to congregate in clusters and comment on each other. Bernard Beitman describes these clusters as "meta-coincidences": "A pair of coincidences, usually occurring within a short time window, in which the content of one coincidence is directly related to the content of the other." In this final chapter, I will talk about three of them: the transformation of the dinosaur egg, the smiles of golden lilies, and the riddle dream about my safety.

The Dinosaur Egg

Kenny invited a group of friends to come and paint at a park by the sea. We had coffee at the Hermosa Café, then walked to the sea at 4:00 pm. The park was new to me, and it was also the first time I had painted outdoors. There are boardwalks at the harbor front, a lawn area, benches and shelters. The most eye-catching is the 100-meter-long breakwater, where a giant ventilation shaft stands at the end of the promenade overseeing the harbor. The shaft is like a dinosaur egg, head uppermost, 30 meters high, with tubes coiling all over the oval-shaped sci-fi structure. It instantly made me think of the three-headed dragons in my dream two years ago.

For a week or so I had been thinking about bringing the dream symbol of the dragon together in a mandala with the symbol of the sacrificial lamb. These two dream symbols have been mysteriously unfolding themselves in my everyday life over the past two years, and were especially conspicuous in my meditation in recent months. I wanted to see whether a visualization of both of them might help move the dreams forward.

Now, in front of me was an oval-shaped structure. I didn't yet know what it was. Kenny made a call, and was told that it is the big ventilation shaft of the Victory Bypass. The tunnel goes right under the seabed and the shaft lets air in and out of the tunnel. It occurred to me that these scenes resembled those of my dragon dream, in which I went from a subway tunnel out to open water, then a boat ride to the other side of the harbor, met the dragons, escaped into another tunnel and entered a big train station for home. The shaft in front of me is an exit as well as an opening to a tunnel with heavy traffic.

The time was around 5:00 pm and the setting sun hung right next to the heart of the dinosaur egg. It added up. In a split second I made up my mind what I was going to paint: dragons sitting on a big watch tower, looking over the city. Amid fears and conflict, the sacrificial lamb offered peace and reconciliation to the people. The ventilation ducts became the bodies of the serpents. At the fringe of the shaft were the dragon heads, the sun radiating at the center of the shaft. The head of the sacrificial lamb was to be sketched onto the sun in a simple outline.

By the seaside, we were able to secure a bench with a table so that our paints, brushes, palettes, small water jars and painting paper could be amply spread out. People were curious, some took photos of us, some chatted with Kenny. I was all in, focusing on the lines, shapes, and movements of the colors.

It was late afternoon, a bit hazy at first, but as the sun set, the color of the sky changed moment by moment, from grayish white to a hint of blue, and suddenly a glorious conflagration of maritime blue, blazing red, and yellowish orange. When I stopped painting and looked up, I was amazed by the panoramic sky in royal purplish red. It was sacred.

Peace amid Fear

My painting was only half done when we left the park. I continued the unfinished work at home. It was relatively easy to visualize the fear-provoking dragons, but it was difficult to convey the paradox of vulnerability and strength in the sacrificial lamb. I drew dragons in tangible shapes and colors, but drawing the lamb superimposed onto the sunlight was elusive. It could only be expressed by suggestion and contrast.

I was tense applying the colors. It didn't work well. I took a break. Then I realized that my difficulty wasn't about painting. I was struggling with a contemplative process to interact with my dream symbols. Paying less attention to working out the sunrays, I tried to reach for my feelings and let them flow through my paintbrush. The image of the lamb in the sun gradually materialized in front of my eyes. When I put some final touches to shade and edges, it felt right.

The painting, resting on the table in my study, was a combination of the two dreams. I could see the delicate symbols with my eyes, surreal, but firmly anchored in my waking life. It was inspired by the breakwater, the bold shaft, and the setting sun at the seaside park. For hours I immersed myself in this composite image of the sun, the dragon and the sacrificial lamb.

A storm was coming. Outside the balcony, strong gusts of wind whipped through the trees. Patchy rain showers pattered against the leaves, sounding like intermittent drum rolls. The storm came as a surprise; it was November, our dry season. The sunset was magnificent two days ago at the park, now the overcast sky sent us back to monsoon season. The air was weird, with a lovely spaciousness and the smell of imminent rain. I closed my eyes and grounded myself in meditation. Time stood still. It was like a dream.

I see scenes from different times. I am in a spiritual realm of life, light, and love. Amid fear, animosity, and suffering, I am home. There is a space deep inside me, calm and still. In my previous dreams I went through the cattle farm, the choppy sea, met the ferocious dragons, and arrived at the train station, not knowing whether to flee or to return, to leave or to find my way home. On the platform at the train station, I hold the sacrificial lamb, clean and neat, calm and peaceful. The lamb has surrendered itself, vulnerable but faithful, with the strength of the glowing sun.

I arrive at Plum Village, the refuge for lost souls, the home for seekers, the basecamp for reaching out to the unsettling world. Plum Village is the altar for the peace offering, the fruition of my mission to offer the sacrificial lamb. Limpid light clarifies the heart and mind of the devoted, to see life in the sacrifice, peace despite fears, hope when there is no hope in sight. The peace offering is for those suffering from the tyranny of fear, pain, torture, illness, tragic loss and death. The peace offering is also bestowed upon those invoking fear, inflicting suffering, administering pain, and plotting tragedies. Dragons are terrifying, but they follow their primitive instinct and are spiritually unconscious of what they are doing. Hating the dragons won't bring peace. Compassion and forgiveness are freeing me from the bondage of grievances, from my own wrongdoings, from the victim mentality of my injured ego. And I am freed from the thirst for justice in an unjust world. I know the pain, the injustice, the suffering. I know them by heart. I choose to forgive, to love, and live in peace.

Memories reappear as if I am watching them again in front of my eyes: my meditative prayer on the roof of the seminary dormitory in 1982, my out of body experience in 1996, and my awakening in front of the camphor tree on a hot summer day half a year ago. There is an indescribable openness. It is like home, one of light and love.

The painting was expressed in a magnificent sunset, then and now. I saw the blazing sky at the park by the sea two days ago, the cheering people under the Tiger Ridge in my meditation,

Constance's precognitive dream, and in the photo exhibition I visited, the same purplish sky. And most importantly, on November 7th last year, when my beloved cat, Mui, passed away, I saw this same sky lit up by the setting sun. Gorgeous was the purplish red, astounded by awe were the people who witnessed that dreamy display of color in every corner of the city. Triumphing over the vulnerability and ephemerality of earthly life is the surrendering lamb and the all-embracing sun.

The Relapse

As I mentioned earlier, Constance's menstruation has been normal again since March 2022, two months after her pet frog dream in that January. You could call it a precognition, as if the dream was foretelling an improbable future event. For us it was a small miracle. When hope had withered, something larger told us not to lose hope. You could also interpret it as a signal that the body already knew beforehand that there was a recovery coming, that it was not precognition but an early bird singing in a voice unfamiliar to our rational minds. Before we knew, the recovering body had already sent out a message which appeared in the form of a frog in Constance's dream. Anyhow, regardless of whether it is a precognition or an early signal of recovery, it is an enigma coded in a mythical language which needs some mindful attention to decode. The image of a frog, ancient symbol of regeneration and fertility, was summoned to the present to serve as a messenger.

Constance's breasts had shrunk in her seven years of "menopause". Now, with her menstrual cycle restored, they have returned to normal. She needed to visit the bra shop again.

"You can't figure out your size?" patiently asked the saleslady, carefully adjusting the bras Constance was trying on. "Honey, your bra doesn't fit at all." She was puzzled, wondering why Constance, like a teenager at puberty, didn't know what was happening to her body. In fact, Constance, now

34, still looks like a high school kid. She ended up buying a couple in her old size.

Her nutritionist had warned that her menstruation would be intermittent for quite a long while before it would stabilize, but in fact her period has been regular every month since the start; it is literally like her second puberty. However, after six months or so, our initial optimism had turned upside down; a big storm seemed to have gathered strength. Constance started gaining weight, month by month, to a point that she cannot tolerate, and so her eating disorder started to return strongly.

To the day of writing, every month around her period, Constance is anxious and feels as if her body is exploding. In her words, she has swollen like a balloon. She keeps hearing a distressing voice telling her she is obese, "fat as hell". She receives a whole lot of bodily messages: her bra is choking her, her face is fat and round, the reflections of her own image on every shiny surface are alarmingly huge. She is as big as a supersized SHE-HULK. Of course, Teresa and I don't see the SHE-HULK in her, but the Hulk is there in her disturbed mind. Usually the week before her period her body retains water and she gains weight. It is a normal bodily rhythm, as we see it. It's just that her weight has been on the rise, without any signs of slowing down. Her traumatized self is activated and in full alarm.

There is a voice in her head: "I don't want to be seen. I should quit my job. If I agree to go hiking with my friends to the Haven Reservoir Park, with my mega-ton body, I would tramp the trails and crack the dam."

These exaggerated objections resemble what was happening when Constance was in deep depression a few years ago. I recall the vicious cycles of expectation and frustration; every time a new method of weight control failed she sank into deeper despair. This time we were so hopeful at the beginning, but in just a few months our moods have swung to the other extreme. Her anguish hit her hard, carrying the weight of all her previous dismay.

She says that all is futile. No matter how hard she tries – dieting, exercising, following the advice of so many proven gurus and medical doctors – nothing good is happening. She is on the brink of a life-threatening relapse. Her inner *firefighter* is screaming, "I want to end it all." I sense a dark force pulling me into the abyss of her desperation. There is a chilling sensation in my spine. It is a familiar feeling. My fear is not new. It's as if I have gone back to the rooftop where Constance was standing four years ago.

In IFS therapy, the term *firefighter* refers to the acute form of a defense mechanism, the most extreme of which would be the ending of suffering by ending one's life. I remember vividly one weekend, in the worst stage of her relapse, I tried to use an IFS technique to take care of her *firefighter*. I said to her, "There is a part of you..." Before I could finish my sentence, she yelled, "Don't talk about this nonsense anymore. I am me. There are no other parts. I want to end it all."

I was dismayed, totally defeated. Constance had poked about among my skills and tools and torn them wide open. IFS, Focusing, EMDR, dreamwork, none of these were working. I was speechless.

Four years ago, when she phoned me from the rooftop, she was weak. I could barely hear her. This time she is strong, speaking with a power and a will that challenges my faith and goodwill. I know that those in deep depression are less likely to gather the strength to end their life, but that when the medication is effective, the initial getting better stage is dangerous because they do have the willpower and physical agility to actualize their death wish. This tiny piece of knowledge chills me to the bone.

One evening, as we walked side by side at the waterfront, her *firefighter* confronted me head on. "If I had a gun, I would put a bullet in my head!" For half an hour I walked alongside her in silence. I didn't have a word to say. I had nothing more to offer. I didn't have any clue how to move on. The only thing I could do was surrender, accept what was happening, and acknowledge the fact that sometimes there is nothing one can do. I entrusted myself to the moment. I rested my eyes on the moon and the stars up in the sky, and the vast, silent sea beside us. I had to accept my incompetence in rescuing my daughter at this crossroads... My only help, if any, was God's good grace.

There was a subtle change in me. I gradually regained my equanimity,– not with a magic wand, but by accepting life as it is. There was calmness, a space for me to clear my mind. I sensed the pull of Constance's desperation. Her *firefighter* was pulling me towards its extreme, that there was no hope, a dead end was the only possible end. A mindful indifference to her death wish helped me to stay away from that sickening pull. I dwelled in the capacious space in which there was empathy and love. My equanimity seemed to have softened her destructive impulse. There was a deep silence. We felt the mutual effect of grounding in the here and now.

When there was a shared calmness between us, I told her, "I am always here for you, by your side." Tears rolled down our faces. We didn't know what would be ahead of us. We are both at the crossroads. We have each other.

Surrender

I surrendered, but that doesn't mean I was not doing anything. I gathered the courage to take an intrusive approach to Constance's dietary treatment. I knew it was unusual for me to call her dietitian directly, but I called anyway, informing her of the dire situation. Based on the symptoms that I listed, she was quick to discern that Constance had to be experiencing a hormonal upsurge: the swelling sensation of her breasts, the weeklong menstruation, the exceptional volume of discharge

... She responded with a substantial change in Constance's meal plan: no dairy products, soya milk or tofu, and stop taking Chinese nutrient soups. All of these, which are good for restoring menstruation, stimulate hormonal production, which induces substantial weight gain in preparation for pregnancy.

At the height of the hormonal upsurge, Constance's body sent her a whole lot of antagonistic signals which she had long forgotten. And the neuro-relic of her depression was riding on these waves of menstrual sensation, pushing her into an emotional tumult. This is the unconscious complex at work, and Constance was trapped inside her past traumatic reflexes, which are like a vortex sucking everything into its abyss. I believe that it is her past traumas riding on all her bodily distresses that trigger this sudden blast.

Constance stopped all dairy intake. The swelling of her body receded a little but she still gained weight, though more slowly. She is still on edge. I am also influenced by her mood swings. Eckhart Tolle pointed out that insisting on the expectation of the mind is the source of pain. When what happens now is contrary to what is expected, there is what he calls a pain-gap; the more the mind insists, the more the suffering. This is what I was, and still am, experiencing. I desperately hope that her weight shows some signs of dropping – a fraction of a kilo would help – so as to defuse the bomb inside her head. This is my secret wish, but the minute I notice it, I let it go. I am mindful not to fall into this pain-gap again. Her uterus had frozen for too long, now her body needs to find the balance of her restored hormonal cycle. Not even her dietitian is sure when that new balance can be reached. What I can do is surrender myself and entrust Constance to the natural rhythm of her body, and to the bigger force from above. It is not my learning, nor my talent that is of service. It is the providence of the divine.

Looking back over the past few years, I have experienced guidance and meaningful coincidences, giving me courage to sail through uncompromising waves. There is a sureness in my heart. I let go of my desire for Constance's recovery to happen at the pace set in my mind. Her wellbeing is beyond my control. I surrender to the moment and stay beside her with empathy and love. I let her negative energy pass through me. I leave it behind me.

The Golden Lilies

Constance wanted to visit her grandpa's grave. Following the Chinese tradition, our extended family visit the graveyard once a year during the Ching Ming Festival in April. But this is winter. Constance took a day off and asked me to drive her there. The graveyard is up a hill and there is no public transport. It is a one-way drive, along the ridge of Blossom Hill. She brought a bunch of golden lilies with her, which she thought grandpa would be happy to see. The dozen flower buds were all full, but not yet open. Pretty were these opal-shaped buds, with tightly closed petals in thin outlines of bright yellowish orange.

Constance had a special bond with her grandpa. When she was little, he used to walk her to school every day, and he'd bring a little wildflower to greet her after school. He often carried her on his shoulders on the way home, and she would hold the stalk of the small white flower in one hand, while the other clung to his bald head. At that time Teresa and I were busy at work. We focused our attention on other aspects of our daughter's life, like schooling, weekend activities, and the friends she made. But my father took good care of Constance's psychological needs. I only recently discovered that my father was dear to her heart. She felt her grandpa's unconditional love. She once told my father that she could feel the presence of spirits, and according to her recollection, he told her not to tell anyone and gave her an understanding smile, as if to say he also had that ability. They kept it as a shared secret. My father had given her a home where her troubled heart would rest. Grandpa's cheerful smile is always in her mind.

It was nice talking over her memories with grandpa while we were cleaning up the graveyard. We placed the lilies in the marble grave vase. The golden color of the flower buds matched grandpa's smile perfectly, Constance whispered to herself. But we both wanted to see those buds blossom. We decided to pay another visit a few days later.

My Father's Smile

In the morning, Constance went to see her dietitian. I stayed home. Just from her text message – the bald figure of 0.5 kilo weight gain in two weeks – I could feel her agitation. It has been on the rise for almost six months, with a net gain of 5 kilos.

In my morning meditation I felt her agitation. It took a while for me to let it pass and rest myself in tranquility. In my contemplation, my father appeared, so did the lilies. It was a surreal vision of a microcosm from inside a flower bud, enveloped by yellowish orange light, a long pistil and several shorter stamens, fresh and alive. My father was wearing a cheerful smile. I felt odd, for my father rarely smiled at me in his lifetime. I knew he was fond and proud of me, but he didn't show it. His smile in my vision came as a pleasant surprise. Everything was in the embrace of the big petals, full of life and energy. I felt like I was inside the same flower buds standing by my father's grave. A clear message was given to me from the golden lilies, but I couldn't put it into words. There was a sureness that Constance's body was pacing out its own rhythm, like the lily that was about to blossom. This insight was timely. It reminded me to let nature take its course, but not to bundle Constance's wellbeing with reducing her body weight to a specific number of kilograms dictated by her. This bundling is her obsession. I almost fell prey to her stubborn drive over weight control. Standing by her side as a companion, it is tempting to yield to her burning desire to lose weight, but in fact, staying calm myself is the only thing that I should do. The golden lily is a reminder to put my trust in the magic of life itself.

By My Father's Grave

Constance and I walked down the stone steps to my father's grave in the sunshine. It had been dry and sunny for a few days. A bit anxious about whether they would have withered, I was delighted to catch sight of the lilies blossoming in the distance.

This time we had brought some tools, a small shovel and a hay knife to clear the weeds and prune the thickets blocking the view. When all was done, we had a seat by the grave to take a rest. From the hillside where we sat, the view of the vast Sandy Bay spread before us. An uplifting panorama it was. The island-dotted sea was shimmering in bright sunlight. The lilies were smiling.

Constance was in a good mood and started to tell again a story she was very fond of. A few months after my father died, she had dreamed of her grandpa sitting on a big rock, smiling, with an ice cream cone in his hand. It made her feel grandpa was telling her not to worry, that he was fine and happy. Six months later, when Constance was hiking with a group of friends and got lost, she came to a spot which, according to her, was exactly the place where she had met grandpa in the dream; the big rock, the stand-alone tree, the bend of the trail, all looked the same. She had been there, that was the feeling. Déjà vu. She was now pointing at a basin not far from the grave where she had found the boulder. It was near where we were sitting. I had heard this story before, of course, but hearing it once again, I was still amused by the ice cream cone and my father's cheerful smile.

It was a good time for me to tell Constance about what I had experienced in my meditation. My father's smile harmonized with the golden color of the petals; the cheerful mood was infectious. The choice of those lilies was a perfect match. I have been filling up gaps in my memory of my father's life. I didn't really have a strong emotional bond with him. I was grateful for having been raised by such a dutiful gentleman with a mild and pleasant temperament, but I restricted myself to the role of a dutiful son in return. I had been so occupied with myself that I failed to connect with him all through my life. To me, he was a traditional Chinese man who didn't talk much about his feelings, not even to his most beloved family. But now I know that he had had a wonderful time with his granddaughter in his last years. Apparently he laughed a lot with Constance, he was happy, he opened himself up to her. In a recent meditation, he was generous in sharing his cheerful smile with me too. It was not faint imagination or a flickering image, it was an embodied feeling; in those cheerful years when he was taking care of Constance he was most contented with what life had bestowed on him.

The more I dwell on this embodied feeling, the more I am thankful to my father for giving her his much needed love when she was a disturbed child. I am also grateful to Constance that her charm and naivety gave my father a sense of completion in his life. It feels like I have found a missing part in my relationship with my father: a substantial actualization of me as a son, a newfound bonding with him, years after his death.

We were sitting side by side, enjoying the winter sun. The golden lilies, petals wide open, invited us to a world of light, life and love. Sunlight glittered through the mounds of silver grass. Tears rolled down Constance's cheek. We heard the chirping of birds in the far distance, a touch of serenity, connecting Constance, my father and me.

The Scar of a Cut-off Breast

The vision of the blossoming lilies tells me a lot about the rhythm of life. The lilies don't talk. The petals open, stamens thrive. Life doesn't need any wordy persuasion. I don't know whether the lily vision is meant for me or for Constance. I just know it is asking me to live and let live, and it is inviting Constance to go with the flow of the body and follow its own timing.

After the visit to my father's grave, I recall Constance's other dream, when she dreamed of the frog. During our evening walk, we revisited that dream once again. In her high school there was a girl, Vicky, who was good-looking and hugely popular, and from a similar middle-class background as Constance. As a newcomer she was a magnet among the students, and especially, among the well-off boys. Constance and Vicky were good friends, buddies, but also opponents in the popularity stakes. Vicky was the newbie in the spotlight, much more popular than Constance. In that "contest," Vicky won. They parted bitterly and have never spoken to each other since graduation.

After so many years, Vicky suddenly appeared in Constance's dream in January, around the same time as her pet frog dream. No more rivalry, Vicky just wanted to spend a few hours with Constance, honestly, as a friend, and without competition. She was frail, thin like a piece of paper. In the dream she was a breast cancer victim with only a few months left in her young life. When they met, the first thing she did was to unbutton her shirt and show her mastectomy. The scar was strikingly recent.

As Constance recalled this dream the scar had invoked intense fear in her. Now she confronted the dream afresh. I did the usual drill, invited her to say hello to her fear, be friendly, and have her fear stay at a safe distance. When Constance was calm, I asked her to reach for the felt sense of the scar again. "The scar is so real..." she murmured. "Vicky just wants to save the trouble of explaining. Showing the scar is a direct way of saying, *This is my cancer. I have already accepted it. I am not going to live.*"

My hunch is that it is a dream about femininity, the withering of female breasts. In her dream, Vicky the opponent was Constance herself in palatable camouflage. Vicky was bidding farewell, her breasts cut off, her life fleeing. She dropped her defensive weaponry, no more wheeling and dealing. She just wanted to be honest with Constance and say a decent goodbye. Now, in hindsight, it can be seen as a farewell to Constance's shrunken breasts before the actual return of her menstruation.

I asked Constance to tell Vicky (the dream persona) what had been happening in the past few months. In Constance's mind, Vicky said to her, "Your breasts could be annihilated like mine, all of a sudden. Take good care of your body."

Constance recalled her dream frog too. Before, it was very fragile; and now the frog has recovered. I asked her, "How is the frog?" She replied, "He is a chill frog. He is happy, sitting on the lily pad. There is nothing to worry about. I have tended to him well. All is well."

There is a sense of matching and fitting, of the psychic undercurrents and the objective repercussions, the bidding farewell to withering breasts, and the growing strength of a chill frog. Both dreams preceded the return of Constance's menstruation, foretelling her physiological transformation as well as the return of her feminine figure. Now we know the frog dream and the cancer dream worked as a pair, yin and yang, a dual precognition.

Her past traumas have been printed in her neuro-circuitry. Her body keeps the score. Now she must unlearn the past and familiarize herself with the language of the frog.

The Riddle Dream, a Meta-Coincidence

Exactly on my 35th wedding anniversary, I woke with a dream that I immediately felt had significance, and had the urge to write it down. It was a vivid and elaborate dream.

- Scene 1. I am attending a church service inside the chapel of a university in the United States. A group of K-Town international students are sitting with me in the front pew. A Caucasian pastor asks us to sit at the back, so we do. People are coming in, filling up the pews. A preacher from K-Town starts the service in the Hakka dialect. He is clumsy and soft spoken. It is boring. I feel sorry for the pastor who has to sit tight besides the Hakka-speaking guy and endure an hour of mumbling in a language he doesn't understand. I sneak out.
- Scene 2. Right outside the chapel door is an arc-shaped platform where armored trucks have parked side by side, so close to each other that I can't make my way out. The pathway is completely blocked. I can go nowhere, so I sit idly on the platform waiting for the service to end. Suddenly a squad in full gear rushes in. Masked guys with rifles in their hands stand shoulder to shoulder, staring at me. There are dozens of them, Caucasian, circling around me, gawking. Unable to figure out why I am chilling out there slothfully, they leave me alone, break into the church and shoot randomly. At first, I think they are here to protect, but they've come to kill. I don't witness the bloodshed, or hear the gunshots. I just know. I peep in from my safe pavilion and see a deserted chapel hall, with a few people, thinly dispersed, hiding behind pews. A faint scream can be heard. I have doubts whether this is really a mass shooting, but I sense that the incident is all over the news. I feel the heaviness of the tragedy. Strangely for me, no panicking, no anxiety. I am at ease.
- Scene 3. I attend another church gathering, much more informal, with a table in front of an audience. My friend Edward is sitting there, painting. Then he performs a strange ritual, asking a random guy from the audience to

pull a small piece which has been torn from the painting out of a bag, which is supposed to be the true meaning of my dream. A big cheer from the crowd when the guy successfully pulls a piece out; it is an image of me walking past a fierce lion. On the side is written a question, "Is Manny safe?"

- Scene 4. After everyone has left, my friend Tammy explains to me how the tiny piece of painting was selected. She brings me to the arc-shaped platform again. There, she shows me a large painting which had been torn into pieces and placed in a metallic dish right on the spot where I was sitting in Scene 2, facing the death squad. A random piece picked from this dish would represent the meaning of my dream. They picked a piece saying, "Manny is safe." They brought the piece to the gathering and asked the guy to pull it out. To their bewilderment, on that preselected piece, "Manny is safe," became, "Is Manny safe?" It came up as a question instead of a definite answer. Tammy said that she and Edward don't really know why. In the dream, I know why. I figured out the answer to the question myself. The answer is not written in words but is shown by what has happened on the spot: the death squad left me alone. After I figured out the answer, Tammy morphs into a woman that I don't know. She has short hair, beige-brown complexion, seems to be from an unknown country with a lot of sunshine. She looks at me for a while without saying a word. She is kind. I wake up.

Edward and Tammy are long-time friends of mine. We met 40 years ago at a Christian fellowship. Now Edward is a professor teaching psychology in San Francisco. He wrote a small book on dreams at a very young age. Tammy is married to Clarence the pastor, also a very good friend of mine.

Obviously, Edward in the dream is not the actual psychology professor in real life but a subpersonality of mine, who interprets dreams and paints. He (I) was concerned about my safety, and drew the lion instead of the three-headed dragon of my previous dream. Edward wanted to believe I would be safe, but he was not sure. He had doubts.

To me, the dream delivers a message loud and clear. It says that despite my (Edward's) skepticism, I will be fine. I was spared by the death squad. But this strong and clear message is expressed in a surprisingly twisted narrative. The mass shooting represents my threat at gun point. Like a set of Russian stacking dolls, the squad becomes a fierce lion in the drawing, which alludes to the three-headed dragon in my previous dream, which, in turn, points to the danger I am facing in real life. The answer to the question of whether I am safe is not told in words. Instead, I am brought to the scene and am invited to ponder the answer myself. The answer was to be found in the strange happening on the arc-shaped platform.

The answer was played out, I could see it in that dramatic situation. There was no need for reasoning, rationalizing or verbal iterating. Peace, I am safe. This is the answer to the question, "Is Manny safe?" The dream message is told in such an unusual, random and bizarre way that is beyond the imagination of a clever novelist.

Even though I was spared in the dream, innocent people were killed; their surviving families were suffering. Recalling the dream, I feel the pain. I feel as if I am an integral part of the suffering whole. We all bear the scars, the agony of crucifixion, the tribulation of our time. My ordeal let me have a taste of the suffering that many are enduring. My narrow escape is not something to be rejoiced in, but a life lesson for me to have faith in the goodness of things and to have compassion for those who are facing adversity in their lives.

At first, Teresa and I planned to invite a few friends who knew about our situation to celebrate our 35th wedding anniversary at home with us. In the end, however, we decided not to. Instead, we had a peaceful meal in a quiet place away from the hustle and bustle of the city. My dream is a timely anniversary gift to both of us. We hope after five years, when things are settled, we will gather all of our beloved friends to celebrate our 40th wedding anniversary and recount the grace in these turbulent years. We look forward to that.

The Loving Kindness of the Mysterious Lady

After dinner, when Constance and I took our leisurely walk by the waterfront, I told her about the dream. She had some new insights: the arc-shaped platform was blocked and I couldn't find a way out, which is similar to my actual situation right now. The beige-brown lady is a distinct racial type, very different from the Caucasians and the K-Town citizens in the dream. She is from a different part of the world, opening a mystery at the end of the dream.

I didn't pay enough attention to this mysterious lady. After discussing with Constance, I revisited the ending of the dream and mindfully attended to the image of the lady. She didn't speak, but I felt that she was saying something to me not in words. She simply looked at me with a kind heart. I could feel her kindness, but I couldn't comprehend what was in her mind. Perhaps she was asking me to trust the message she had delivered through the dream. I can only think about this logically, but I don't have a concrete feeling of her message of peace.

For synchronicity to be convincing, subjective images beg for parallel coincidences in the objective world. The dream, the clever narrative and the perceived peace message are all products from inside my head. I consider the dream as a delightful gift for our anniversary; it could also be wishful thinking too. Deep down I ask, are all these episodes churning out from my imaginative mind? If the dream meant something significant, could there be relevant incidents happening in the objective world? As some kind of a proof, maybe? That it coincided with my anniversary is one. Can there be another to confirm the synchronicity?

Shockingly, something did happen. Again, I got what I asked for. Just when I came back home from my walk with Constance, I received a text from Brian saying that another accountant of the investment company had been interrogated. The timing of this message was surprisingly coincidental. It means that the situation has worsened, which contradicts, head on, the peace message in my dream. I talk to myself, "No, I am still in danger, and the danger is getting bigger." Is this yet another test of faith? To my relief, the fear is much less compared with the previous times, but still, I am worrying. The dream, with its happy ending, looks like irony. Am I safe? There is a sure yes in the last scene of the dream, but the coincidence of the new development reshapes the peace message into a riddle, which propels a deeper exploration into the mystery of the dream.

I made time for meditative Focusing, going back to the crucial moments of the dream. I went deeper into the emotional state when I was sitting on the platform facing the squad. In the here and now, after getting Brian's message, I revisited the scene, and I was calm. I sensed the tautness of the shooters. I could feel the hard metallic surfaces of their rifles. Strangely, I was at ease.

I tried to reach for Edward in the dream. He had been sure of the answer "Manny is safe." But it appeared as a question, without a definite answer. I could sense the ambivalence on Edward's part. He was more on the side of being sure, but he had doubts.

Then I re-visited the last scene. In my meditation, Tammy performed once more the ritual of placing the torn-up pieces of the painting into the metallic dish. I took a closer look. A gleam of sunlight was glowing at the center of the dish; white light shone through pieces of luminous paper which flickered in a gentle breeze. I was at ease in the dream, with a definite answer to the question, but in my meditative state, there was a strange discrepancy: my mind still had doubts, but the answer was solid in the felt sense of the body. The body doesn't think; it is what it feels. I felt safe.

Then I attended to the mysterious lady. I looked into her eyes. She was kind. For the moment, I dropped myself into the dream: I let my worries "float", I observed myself from a calm space. I found steadfast peace. Before, I could vaguely feel the spiritual heart as Adyashanti has described in his book *The Direct Way*. This time, when I placed my awareness at my chest, I had a distinct feeling of the spiritual heart, a connected awareness. It was intimacy without attachment and demand, in a subtle and quiet presence.

This feeling matched the loving kindness I got from the mysterious lady with the beige-brown complexion. She spoke to me without uttering a word. There was a subtle quietness enveloping both of us.

After the meditation, I read Adyashanti again. "The spiritual heart," he writes, "is boundless like the sky and ever-present like the air we breathe. It does not close nor does it open; it is ever-present like awareness, ever expansive like the sky." Whereas the human heart, he writes, "it opens then closes, it loves then hates, it accepts then rejects, it trusts then fears."

Now these descriptions make a lot of sense to me. Yes, there is a difference between the human heart and the spiritual heart. It is exactly the kind of discrepancy I have experienced: I feel anxious when I think of the threat, but at the same time I feel peace when I rest myself in a meditative state. From the vantage point of my spiritual self, the inner awareness, the human heart is observable and describable. Its emotions, ambitions and commotions flicker all the time. Resting in the spiritual heart, the ebb and flow of the human heart can be contained. When emotions are observed and described, they are less dominating and can be kept at bay.

The dream has a twisted narrative but the message is straightforward. Is Manny safe? Manny is safe. However, when I go deeper, behind the straightforward message, there is more. Something profound, much more essential than the question of safety. It is the practice of existential trust.

I brought these insights with me to the hiking trails, sunny was the day. I rested myself in the vastness of the sky and the stillness of the mountains. Yes, my human heart is full of minuscule thoughts all the time and occasionally big waves of emotion. But after many trials and tribulations, the spiritual heart is within my reach. Of course, some devotion and attention are required, but its steadfast calmness is always there for me.

On the way downhill, I took a rest beside a gently whispering stream. The water was clear and serene; the ambiance was intimate and sublime. I closed my eyes and saw a wide array of emotions, like ripples and eddies, one replacing the other incessantly if I let them feed on my attention. But if I moved my awareness away from them, they were as transient as water streaming through my fingers. I thought of some friends who have been hit by acute sickness, and of others who have passed away in recent years. I thought of Constance's recovery, and her little talk with the trees. I thought of the golden lilies and my father's smile. The question, "Am I safe?" is irrelevant. My peace rests on the spiritual heart, not on whether I am safe and not experiencing misfortune. Of course, we pray for goodness and mercy, but the fact is that one way or the other, pain and suffering will find their way into our life. Even for those lucky ones who live a peaceful life, death is an inevitable finale.

The riddle dream, and the coincidences that followed, all come together as a graduation ritual. The message of peace is not manifested in my fortunate escape, but in the kindness on the messenger's face. Kindness is here already, irrespective of the fragility and vulnerability of human existence. My spiritual heart, with its expansive vastness, is spacious enough to hold my human heart. Peace doesn't depend upon what would happen to me in the months to come. Peace is securely anchored in the here and now. Kindness is all around me, its sureness is embedded in Constance's cheerful smile, the tenderness of Teresa holding my hand, and the abundant grace given to me in times of trials.

Epilogue: Synchronicity, Dreamwork, and Focusing

What have I learned from my spiritual journey so far? What generalizations can be drawn from my experiences in dreams, synchronicity, and the ramifications of my awakening?

Steve Taylor, a lecturer and researcher in the UK, interviewed 61 people alleged to be experiencing an awakening and categorized them into three types: those born with that sensitivity, those who cultivate it with continued spiritual practices, and those who are enlightened in the midst of intense emotional turmoil. His cases were mostly of the third type, people whose egos were beaten up by trauma, cancer or other kinds of tragedies; the thick egoic wall crumbled, secular pursuits withered, protective shields were pierced open and they began to hear the whispering of nature, the breathing of living souls around them, and the beating of their own heart.

My case is obviously of the third category. But I guess, inside me there are some elements of the first and second. Constance is sensitive to spiritual beings, as am I, but much less so. We were born with it. I guess my father, Constance's grandpa, had it too.

Before my unannounced awakening, I had already been practicing Focusing and meditation for a few years. Seen in hindsight, I had twice entered a trance state in which there was no time and space. These two episodes occurred to me as preparatory steps leading to the moment of my awakening before the giant camphor tree.

At first, I didn't even think of it as such, it was perhaps just another meditative experience like the other two in which I was in a trance. The word awakening came to me later when I read Eckhart Tolle's *The Power of Now* and Taylor's book *Extraordinary Awakenings: When Trauma Leads to Transformation*. I found that what had happened to me was similar to what many others described in their books.

Now, seen from a distance, it was as Steve Taylor says. At that time the emotional turmoil was so overwhelming that my egoic shell was shattered and cracked open. Light shone through. I had a glimpse of blissful calmness in the state of being interconnected with all there is.

However, the ramifications have been surprisingly contradictory. Changes have been drastic and there is a shift in my consciousness, but life is mundane as usual with the ego still active. Here to stay is the major shift of awareness that there is a good self, a divine calmness, inside me, which is uniquely me and, yet, a part of the whole. As a result, the activities of the ego have been much more discernible and adjustable; its ambitions to achieve, to conquer, to be recognized, have diminished to such an extent that defeat, losing face, misfortune, and suffering are less concerning. Previously big egoic rushes now appear trivial and insignificant. Love, courage, authenticity, empathy, and connectivity become the anchor of daily life.

However, awakening has not superseded the banality of life. At first, I expected peace of mind most of the time. But, on the contrary, I have experienced no fewer challenges, doubts, desolation, fatigue, anxiety, and fear. Gradually I realize that these are purges and trials to help me bring my awakening into my everyday life. To stay awakened is a lifelong journey, not a peak experience once and for all. There are some preparatory steps to take before, and there are plenty of nitty-gritty things to learn along the journey. My spiritual journey has been "thickly" embedded in meaningful coincidences, as described in the pages of this book.

Synchronicity

Earlier in my life I didn't know the word synchronicity. Memorable coincidences happened only sparingly throughout my life. I hadn't experienced any strange coincidences and even if I had, I was not receptive to them. However, in the past two years, synchronistic coincidences have become much more frequent, and they tend to cluster around critical moments in crises and challenges.

Synchronicity is a significant gateway to my spiritual growth. Selective attention, self-fulfilling prophecy and such, all these handy explanations just can't write off the improbable incidents that have been flooding into my life.

Most of my previous research projects were ethnographic in nature. In order to get to know a particular group or community, I would spend weeks and months with them, observing their interactions and participating in their daily routines. Ethnography is in fact a process of self-reflection; the ethnographer's own reflexivity is the research tool for measuring results. It is most fruitful when the values and worldview of the ethnographer conflict with the group s/he is researching. When there are discrepancies there are possibilities of new findings and thus new knowledge.

Experiencing synchronicities is like doing ethnographic research. I have to adjust my conceptions of reality in order to accommodate new experiences, which don't make sense if I cling to my previous understanding of the world. Synchronicity points to some form of choreographing, whose impacts we feel without knowing the logic of its operation. In my previous projects, I had dived into the communities of underground bands in K-Town, worked inside a bar to see how Western culture was cultivated in a developing city in the rural part of the country, stayed in a toy factory to see how rural workers were acquiring an urban way of life. I was quite confident in mapping the cultural logic in these groups of people when the time I stayed with them was long enough.

My spiritual journey has been embedded in synchronicity. I can only appreciate the effects on me on the receiving end, but its inner workings remain unfathomable. As an ethnographer, the only thing I can do is to faithfully apprehend the effects on myself, make sense out of the process, and record the recordable. But there is always a veil that we can't pierce through, a mystery that we can't decipher, and a bigger web of things that is beyond our reach.

I gave some initial thoughts on synchronicity in Chapter 5. Here, I will draw from my experiences and reflections and come up with some generalizations that may be of benefit to readers in life situations different from mine.

First, there are certainly some unseen dynamics or configurations at work in the space between the physical and the subjective worlds. The I Ching, Carl Jung's archetypical symbols, telepathic communication, inspirations from Mother Nature, the energy stored in and released from our unconscious, the symbolism of dreams – all of these point to some unseen links in what can be called the in-between space, between individuals, between humans and other beings. The I Ching is a case in point. This ancient body of collaborative texts works on a delicate balance between simplicity (the basics of yin and yang) and mathematical complexity (derivatives of the 64 hexagrams). Divination for a particular person in a particular situation is rolled out by sheer randomness (drawing sticks or tossing coins). As Jung pointed out, the I Ching has its own operating configuration that is in obvious contrast to the logic of causality and rationality. The operation of the I Ching is meticulously crafted, but it is difficult to lay bare the inner workings of the divination process. The ancient Chinese emphasized practicality over comprehensibility. The working assumption is that there are patterns of inter-connectedness between people and happenings.

These patterns are abstracted and generalized in the 64 hexagrams and can be applied to individuals across time and space. I don't practice I Ching divination, I just experience its effects on the receiving end, which has given me a strong sense of synchronicity. It seemed to me that I could almost feel the presence of a web of forces linking a cluster of images, words, thoughts, feelings and concrete happenings around my life at the particular point when hexagrams 53 and 8 were divined for me, right before my awakening. The sense of that interconnected web has been there in all the other synchronistic experiences I have had, regardless of whether it was a materialized dream, a missed phone call or the encounter of a mythic symbol, I feel the presence of that web somewhere in between my very existence and the world around me.

Second, synchronicity is imbued with meanings to be apprehended and actualized by the experiencer. Like an invitation, synchronicity is meaningful only if it is actively engaged; it will recede into banality if it remains unnoticed. The cases documented in this book meant a lot to me. They have invited me into a vast terrain of meaning and purpose. More often than not, they have been here to facilitate my psychological and spiritual growth, like Jung's well-known case of the scarab beetle, which helped his client shake off her rational defense and allowed a therapeutic breakthrough. There were a few occasions in which I was in distress, and something came along to teach me how to find peace. In other instances, coincidences came in the form of advice on what to do or not do next. The element of surprise in synchronicity loosens up normal routines, which allows new insights to emerge. When I painted with my friends at the park by the sea, the mythic symbols in my dreams and meditations converged in the things I saw on the spot. It was a summation of synchronicities, layer upon layer, intertwined with my life stories. The actualization of the painting in which the sacrificial lamb shines through the tyranny of the dragons is a representation of my deep realization of peace amid terror, blessing in the disguise of pain.

Third, with synchronicity, time and space are fluid and flexible. Our everyday lives are locked within the linearity of time and space, but synchronicity operates in a dimension where these are not limiting factors. Candice didn't know me when she made the divination. What was in the scripts and what was happening in my life were in a different time and space. Candice's intuition seems to have penetrated these planes when she tossed the coins. The hexagram hinted at my daughter's menstrual restoration, and advised me to abort my travel plan. I was told, in the form of ancient metaphors, what was happening in my here and now. The precognitive elements of my dream also pierce through time, crisscrossing my dreamy unconscious (a peace offering) and the physical world (the death of my cat). I dreamed of a three-headed dragon, the meaning of which gradually unfolded over a year and a half. Ancient myth entered Constance's dreams, defying space. My awakening was a state without time and space. I was simply there, connected to the vastness of the sky. These bits and pieces of synchronistic events point to the permeability of happenings in the past, the present and the future.

Fourth, a difficult question: is there a bigger consciousness beyond us? Synchronicity presumes a sentient being(s) instigating coincidences. For social scientists, this is an unproven hypothesis; it is way over the top. It breaches the disciplinary boundary of empirical research and enters the realms of philosophy and theology. However, the ethnographic evidence thrown upon me requires an honest probing into the hypothesis of a sentient presence. God is too restrictive a naming, carrying contradictory notions in different institutionalized religions. The empirical side of my case doesn't negate the possible existence of God, or the belief in Jesus as the Son of God, or of Muhammad as the Godsent Prophet, and Buddha as the Enlightened One; however, it can't be stretched to a definite yes or no according to a particular faith. An informed presumption would be the existence of a Source that brought about my spiritual and enlightened awareness in all the synchronicities I had gone through. I now believe in providence, that I am taken care of. My ethnographic evidence doesn't allow me to go this far. Some sorts of choreographing are evidenced; however, a personal and caring God behind providence is not. Indeed, I have taken a leap of faith, and at the same time I have suspended the naming of the bigger consciousness beyond us. I now have a better appreciation of the wisdom of the Tao Te Ching: "The tao that can be told is not the eternal Tao. The name that can be named is not the eternal Name."

Fifth, agency. Does an individual's endeavor matter? If I precognize a future, can it be changed by my knowing of it and acting differently? My experiences have taught me that my reactions matter, that they can change the course of events. The I Ching is "the book of changes" – for better or for worse. Good and bad simultaneously exist; when good fortune is full-blown, misfortune is in the corner, and vice versa. This is the philosophy of I Ching. I was advised to stop writing my columns, stay quiet and not leave the city. I followed through. My compliance, I believe, has had consequences.

With synchronicities, I can feel the seemingly unrelated, acausal incidents revolving and interacting with each other. And there is a meaning-making part to the equation. It is I who am astounded by the coincidences, it is I who have a burning desire to make sense of the enigma presented in front of my eyes. As my perception of the situation has changed, my subsequent actions will be changed. And mostly, for me the changes have been in the psychological and spiritual realms. I have been more grounded; some age-old habits have changed; I feel free and peaceful and my relationships with my family and friends have been much more authentic and enjoyable than before. My decision and action might not change the bigger scheme of things, calamity might not be avoided simply by my good will and kind heart, but after my awakening my perception of suffering and misfortune has changed a lot. After all, for me the ultimate concern for this lifetime is spiritual maturity, not striving for a risk-free and painless life.

Dream

What can I say about dreams? I started to work on dreams when I recovered from depression nine years ago. In the few years before and after my retirement, dreamwork helped me a lot in discovering the unknown sides of me, giving me insights into my distorted persona, suppressed needs and emotional blockages. Recurrent dreams are messages from the unconscious persistently telling us about the shadowy sides that we don't accept as part of ourselves. These dreams can be categorized as blockage dreams, which, if worked through, can result in big leaps in personal growth. These blockage dreams are prominent in the dream literature, especially in the field of therapy and counseling, but they are not the kind of dreams I am focusing on in this book. The dreams I have documented here are mostly from different categories. Some of them bring together the personal and the collective, the idiosyncratic and the social. Others have mythic and spiritual symbols that do not originate from personal histories. Some even have precognitive elements and are deepened with synchronicity.

Throughout this book, I have given some thick descriptions of the work I have done on individual dreams, and there are a few observations I would like to bring up here about the corpus as a whole. First, most collective myths are beyond us, but nevertheless, a few might get into our dreams, articulating the personal with the mythic. Previously, the symbolism in my dreams all came from objects, characters and experiences in my everyday life. Over the past two years I started to encounter mythic symbols from outside the life stories of Constance and myself. The frog, the dragon, and the lamb have brought profound meaning to my consciousness. They are all from ancient and spiritual myths. It seems to me that we dwell in a vast pool of cultural resources much bigger than our life, our knowledge structure and our awareness. Sometimes symbols come up without us knowing where they come from and why they enter our dreams. Meanings come about when we are cross-checking and triangulating myths with the happenings in our personal lives. Awakening is not simply a blissful moment of entering into the oneness of all, it is a prolonged process of the merging of the personal and the mythic. An archetypical dream is one of the interfaces. The interplays would be much more intense in times of personal crises and big social changes.

Second, dreams are not self-contained – they are permeable, expansive and evolving, a source of energy to push us forward. After years of initiation, now I am more sensitive to dream symbols and capable of bringing them into my waking life. I invited Constance to bring her pet frog from her dream to a few sessions of Focusing. After some tending and mindful caring, the feeble frog in her dream became a chill-out frog in her heart, comforting her in times of stressful menstruation. The three-headed dragon got into my meditation and my painting; in the process, I have learned to tame my own anxiety associated with the dragon. The sacrificial lamb appeared in one dream, and then came up time and again in another dream, in my meditations, as a tangible object (the body of my cat) and as an inspiration in my spiritual journey. Most importantly, it has become the symbol of a duty given to me, to be a messenger of peace, by living it out in my life.

Third, dreams work with synchronicity and other forms of communication to get the conscious self in contact with the body, the unconscious, and the in-between spaces. There are many signals and messages given to us from various means and channels, dreaming is only one of these. Some people are sensitive to dreams, some receptive to inspiring songs and movies, others might easily find meaning in coincidences. Our rational mind is just a small and restrictive domain of knowing, there is a vast space in between our mind and body, the deep sea of unconscious, and the unfathomable but energetic space in nature. It would be strange if dreams work alone in these realms of exchanges. Life speaks to us in a multiplicity of ways. Now I do dreamwork, Focusing, meditation, painting, contemplation, and reading sacred texts. These practices work for me interchangeably.

Meta-coincidences work with dreams too; dreams and synchronicities comment on and augment each other. The last dream in this book is just such a meta-dream. It comments on my previous dragon dream, reassuring the skeptical me, indicating my safety, and at the same time triggering another paradoxical synchronicity. I received the news of a new arrest, begging me to go deeper into the message of the dream about what peace really means. Then in my meditation, I had a deep realization that my peace rests in my spiritual heart in the here and now, irrespective of whether I will be free of threat in the future. It all happened on my 35th wedding anniversary. There were energetic exchanges between dreams, my waking mind, and tangible events in my life. Things are unfolding, layer upon layer, in meta-coincidences, to hammer home a spiritual lesson for me and my family.

Focusing

Looking back, my inner journey began in 2014 with the intent of getting out of my depression. The practice of Focusing, initiated by Eugene Gendlin, was the first tool I used to heal myself. It was by chance – Liz, my former research student, happened to give me Gendlin's book – that I learned to switch off my rational mind and attune to the felt sense of my body. Focusing is about detecting something I vaguely know but cannot yet say, and without succumbing to logic and rationality, letting that something emerge, like a baby crab crawling cautiously out of its sand hole. Through Focusing, I started to get to know the forgotten sides of me, hiding in the shadows, incompatible with my self-perceived persona, yet nevertheless in sync with the implicit me, waiting there in my unconscious, eager to be seen and heard.

Gendlin's easy-to-follow steps are helpful: 1. Clearing a space, describing inner feelings. 2. Letting the felt sense form, waiting for the murky sensation to reveal itself. 3. Finding a handle, seeing which description would fit it best. 4. Resonating with the handle, matching the handle with the felt sense. 5. Ask but don't answer, wait for the feeling to stir and offer an answer concerning a life situation. 6. Receive the message from the implicit, the internal reservoir yet to be seen, and protect it from critical voices that interrupt.

These steps are basic.

Dreamwork is another way into the uncharted sea of the unconscious and to the mythic realm of the archetypal. Focusing and dreamwork are not antithetical; on the contrary, they facilitate each other. In fact, the symbolism and imagery in dreams are splendid handles for Focusing; turn these handles and doors can be opened and shadows set free. Dreamwork actively bridges our dreams and waking life, carrying us forward stepwise, and after a while small steps become a transforming leap. In Jungian terms, it is a process of life-long individuation.

Focusing is a practice of befriending bodily sensations, with the general aim of personal growth. The late Gendlin refrained from stepping into the realm of spirituality. He held onto the basics, the essential steps of enhancing self-awareness. Speaking from my experience, Focusing could serve as the foundation of dreamwork, meditation, mindfulness and other practices. It is a wild card for a wide range of therapeutic interventions and spiritual experiences.

Ultimately, all inner journeys lead to the understanding of the spiritual self, whether through Focusing, meditation, dreamwork or otherwise. I have ventured into the vast terrain of the unconscious, the myths and symbols in dreams, and my awakening amid the tumult of social change. Holding all these together are some divine powers choreographing synchronicities for my attending soul.

I would like to end this epilogue with the I Ching oracle given to me. The oracle comes with two hexagrams, the first is a general meaning of the process of changes (H53), the second being the projected ending (H8).

My first hexagram is H53: Gradual Progress

The wild goose gradually draws near the cloud heights.

Its feathers can be used for the sacred dance.

For me this book is a flight to cloud heights. The large bird gradually draws near to the high land, from the sea to the spiritual ground, through wind and rain, the feathers that coat the wild goose have gradually transformed. They can be used in a sacred ritual, calling us to surrender, to transcend suffering and to realize our humanity. The sacred feathers of the wild goose have manifested in my life and on the pages of this book.

The second hexagram is H8: Holding Together.

Holding together brings good fortune.

Inquire of the oracle once again

Whether you possess sublimity, constancy, and perseverance;

Then there is no blame.

My initial reading of H8 was focused on the word Yuen (sublimity, or the Source), which I saw as the spiritual experience of my awakening. After I finished the first draft of this book, I read H8 once again. It feels like standing on a watchtower looking back at the journey I have gone through. At the very start, I was thrown into a maze. I could only see tiny bits and pieces of a big puzzle, not knowing what was going to happen next. Now I have trolled through the maze and taken a better look at the whole puzzle. When I *inquire about the oracle once again,* I have a more substantial appreciation of the divination given to me. It is a confirmation of my endeavor and an invitation for me to carry on. It beckons me to keep on possessing *sublimity, constancy, and perseverance.* Yes, I have no more grievances concerning my "misfortune." *There is no blame.* I have faith in the divine.

He gives strength to the weary
and increases the power of the weak.
Even youths grow tired and weary,
and young men stumble and fall;
but those who hope in the Lord
will renew their strength.
They will soar on wings like eagles;
they will run and not grow weary,
they will walk and not be faint.
(The Book of Isaiah 40: 29-31)

A Note on the Editing Process

For anonymity, contextual details have been edited and personal particulars changed. On the other hand, I have recorded dreams and visions as accurately as I can. Spiritual experiences seem ephemeral and malleable, despite their sense of factuality to those experiencing them. They are vulnerable to the intentional or unconscious manipulation of the storytellers to make them look extraordinary. Throughout the writing and editing processes, whenever I had the impulse to dramatize or to enhance the storytelling, I would check against the experiences and bring the narratives back to what had actually unfolded.

On March 26, 2023, while I was proofreading the manuscript, I was hesitant about altering a major event. If I changed its nature to make it a bit ambiguous, I would feel more comfortable. I was undecided. I waited.

I woke up in the early morning on the next day, much earlier than I usually do. I had an elaborate dream before waking, but the only scene I could recall is as follows:

I am in the UK at a photocopying kiosk inside a big building on the waterfront. I have a dozen pages to copy. The Xerox machine is strange. It is a glass window ledge hanging on the edge of the building, facing the seawater below. To make copies, I have to place the papers face down onto the glass surface one piece at a time. The clarity of the print depends on the reflection of the water. I am struggling to make the copies legible. The overcast sky is blueish gray; the sea is unsettling.

I had a vague feeling that this was about my hesitation about blurring some factual details in the manuscript. The dream scene seemed to be of some significance, so I wrote it down in my dream journal right away.

Teresa was still asleep; I didn't want to make too much noise. The blueish sky of early dawn was enchanting. I looked at the bookshelf and picked up Carl Jung's *The Red Book* for a morning read. I had begun to read it six months ago, and had left the book on the shelf untouched since then. I continued reading where I had left off – the bookmark was on page 157 – at a passage in which Jung was arguing with his soul.

Suddenly, there was something red flapping outside the window, just an arm's length from me. It caught me by surprise. Standing on the window ledge was a bird in shocking red, the same colour as the cover of the book. Jung first recorded his visions in his *The Black Books,* then refined and expanded them into *The Red Book.* Here came a red bird with black spots on its wings. I had never seen a red bird in the neighbourhood in my 25 years of living here. And at such close range! How come the bird to be visiting me at this peculiar moment?

Bewildered by the coincidence, I read the page again, hoping to find some clues. Here were the few verses that might have some relevance.

Page 157: Splitting of the Spirit.

... My soul spoke to me saying, "My path is light."

Yet I indignantly answered, "Do you call light what we men call the worst darkness? Do you call day night?"

To this my soul spoke a word that roused my anger: "My light is not of this world."

I cried, "I know of no other world."

The soul answered, "Should it not exist because you know nothing of it?"

I: ".... What is it going to be, if not knowledge? Where is security? Where is solid ground? Where is light? Your darkness is not only darker than night, but bottomless as well. If it's not going to be knowledge, then perhaps it will do without speech and words too?"

My soul: "No words, either."

The red bird stayed on my mind throughout the day. No words. Not of this world, it seemed. Full of life.

The next morning, on March 28, in my meditation I quickly got into a trance state. My awareness was clear and calm. The image of the red bird was vividly here. No words nor thoughts. Fading in and out were images rich in sensations. The coincidences in the past two years appeared as a cumulative whole, not a single event but a collage of events. It was serene.

Right after my meditation, I wrote my journal slowly, pondering my visions, trying to find words to describe what I had seen. I googled the bird; it was a scarlet minivet. The males are red, females are yellow. The sighting yesterday morning had stirred some rich emotions inside me but I could not grasp the latent meaning of this coincidence. I could only think of the bird in hexagram 53, from last year: "The wild goose gradually draws near the cloud heights." As the bird is finishing its journey, its feathers have gradually transformed into a colourful coat. "The feathers can be used in a sacred dance," said the oracle. The scarlet minivet, fluttering its wings in front of the window, gave me feelings of being in a sacred dance.

I took a rest and resumed writing in the afternoon. The scarlet minivet reminded me of Jung's most talked about case of synchronicity, the scarab beetle tapping on the window. As I wrote about this, the red bird pattered on my window again, so close that I was astounded. This time it flew towards me, flapping its wings, contacting the window. I met its eyes, then off it flew. It was surreal.

Twice it came, so timely that I believe it was an incident of synchronicity. I went back to the pages of *The Red Book* that I had read yesterday morning. The soul says: "My path is light. My light is not of this world. It is the path without speech, the light without words."

In *The Red Book*, Jung is transcending the "spirit of the times," and finds his way to the "spirit of the depths." Many Jungians interpret the former as the zeitgeist of the world, the latter the unknown depths of the collective unconscious.

The sequence of events sheds light on the meaning of the scene I had dreamed. The Xeroxing in the dream was done by the light reflecting from the surface of the water. Since the water was rippling, the flickering light rendered the print quite illegible. The Xeroxed pages, dozens of them, all had blank spaces and missing links.

Now I could gradually make sense of all these crisscrossing psychological and physical happenings: they were giving me an answer to the question of whether to edit out some crucial components in this book. My felt sense was a yes. This meta-coincidence was assuring me that it was fine to leave some blank spaces here and there in the manuscript. The red bird sent a message to me not by words, but by the color of its feathers and the timing of its appearance. It was not a random incident of me strolling along the woodland and seeing a bird. The dream, the verses I read from *The Red Book*, the bird flapping its wings before my eyes, the second visit, all synchronized to give me a substantial understanding of the making of this manuscript; its spiritual meanings are embodied in the experiences deep within the soul, not in specific names and places. The focus of attention should not be on the specificity of what is happening in the world, but on the light shining through the sea of the unconscious, so that the magnificent life-forms in the deep oceans could be brought to the attention of the curious mind.

I made the decision to delete some major events in my draft and finished revising the manuscript in the summer of 2023. I then submitted the book proposal to five publishers. I waited for a few months but got no response. *Collective Ink* was the last one on the list that I had prepared. They have the most elaborate submission guidelines which require quite a lot of work. A preferred word count of 40,000 to 60,000 (80,000 max) is set; so I spent a few days trimming my MS from 95,000 to 70,000.

On October 14, 2023, I sent an enquiry to *Collective Ink*. Two days later I had a dream in which I was sitting inside a public library, drafting a few love letters to my wife. I left them on the table as I was about to leave. A lady wearing strange and elegant clothes, handed me back my drafted letters. She had proofread them and they were now in elegantly printed script with neat calligraphic revisions. I was bewildered by this mysterious lady whose attire was so unfamiliar that I believed she was outside my circle of acquaintances. Where did she come from?

Strangely, on October 25, 2023, the scarlet minivet, the one who visited me six months ago, came back again. In March, he had "knocked on" my window and stayed in the neighborhood for two weeks and then left. Now he visited again and did the same thing – flapping his wings against the window of my study. Our eyes met. We were just a meter apart. I was in awe. Six days later, on October 31, 2023, I received an email from *Collective Ink*. One reviewer said: "An excellent book with much for the reader to take away and much that is inspirational. Editorially, however, there are problems, largely due to English not being the author's first language." The other reviewers concurred. They asked me to have a professional editor revise it, and then resubmit.

I had never thought of hiring an editor before receiving this request from *Collective Ink*. On impulse I thought of Rob Foxcroft, the author of the book *Feeling Heard, Hearing Others*. He is a friend of my teacher Ed, who had organized a study group on Rob's book. I asked Ed to see whether Rob would refer a professional editor to work on my manuscript. To my surprise Rob said he would like to read it through himself. I was thrilled and had a hunch that he was the lady in my dream offering me editorial help.

I sent him the manuscript in early November. He replied that he was having some problems with his eyesight, and he looked forward to reading the manuscript. A few months passed without any message from Rob. I patiently waited. But the longer I waited the more anxious I became.

I believed that this book was a response to a divine calling, but the long wait seemed to prove that what I considered a calling was just wishful thinking. I asked myself if the dream of the elegant lady offering me help was just a random thought? Is this project my egoic yearning to work on something meaningful or is it really a calling from the above? I learned a precious lesson by resting these doubts and self-questioning in my prayers and meditations. I found peace by letting go of my wishes and reaffirming my role as a messenger. I put my faith in what I had been experiencing – the dreams, the visions, and the subsequent coincidences recorded in this book. I believe they are meaningfully connected in order to give me guidance one step at a time. I no longer felt anxious to get a yes or no from Rob.

On February 10, 2024, I received an email from Joyce Foxcroft, Rob's wife, saying that Rob's eyesight needs some care, and he is not able to work on my manuscript. She has some spare time and will take on the editing work. I felt grateful. This was like being given a missing piece of the puzzle. After some twists and turns, and a test of faith, what was in the dream turned out to be true. Joyce had carefully proofread the manuscript and sent it to me in June, as the elegantly dressed lady did in the dream.

The editing process had been infused with dreams, meditative visions, visits from the red bird, verses from Jung's *The Red Book* and coincidental happenings in my daily life. Meaningful coincidences are like sacred birds, pattering their wings on the window of my soul. I have experienced wonder, guidance, and loving kindness beyond speech and words.

References

Adyashanti (2021). The Direct Way. Sounds True.

Adyashanti (2014). Resurrecting Jesus: Embodying the Spirit of a Revolutionary Mystic. Sounds True.

Beitman, Bernard (2016). *Connecting with Coincidence: The New Science for Using Synchronicity and Serendipity in Your Life.* Health Communications, Inc.

Beitman, Bernard (2022). *Meaningful Coincidences: How and Why Synchronicity and Serendipity Happen.* Park Street Press.

Cheung, Theresa and Julia Mossbridge (2018) *The Premonition Code.* Watkins Media

Gendlin, Eugene (1986). *Let Your Body Interpret Your Dreams.* Chiron.

Gendlin, Eugene (1978). *Focusing.* Everest House.

Ikemi, Akira (2017). Update Your Listening and Therapy with Focusing: The Fundamentals of Sensing, Speaking and Listening (Chinese edition, Trans. Li, Ming). China Light Industry Press.

Jung, Carl G. (2009). The Red Book: A Reader's Edition. W.W. Norton & Company.

Jung, Carl G. (1989). *Introduction to Jungian Psychology: Notes of the Seminar on Analytical Psychology given in 1925.* Princeton University Press.

Jung, Carl G. (1974). Dreams. Princeton University Press.

Jung, Carl G. (1964). *Man and his Symbols.* Anchor Press.

Kolk, Bessel van der (2014), The Body Keeps the Score*: Brain, Mind, and Body in the Healing of Trauma.* Viking.

Nepo, Mark (2000). *Book of Awakening.* Red Wheel-Conari.

Paul, Annie Murphy (2021). *The Extended Mind: the Power of Thinking Outside the Brain.* Mariner Books.

Savary, Louis et. al. (1984). *Dreams and Spiritual Growth: a Judeo-Christian Way of Dreamwork.* Paulist Press.

Schwartz, Richard C. (1997). *Internal Family Systems Therapy*. Guilford.

Taylor, Steve (2021). *Extraordinary Awakenings: When Trauma Leads to Transformation*. New World Library.

Thich Nhat Hanh (1975). *The Miracle of Mindfulness*. Beacon Press.

Tolle, Eckhart (2005). A New Earth: Awakening to Your Life's Purpose. Dutton.

Tolle, Eckhart (1997). *The Power of Now: A Guide to Spiritual Enlightenment*. Namaste.

About the Author

Manny Mak, PhD, columnist and retired professor. His PhD in communication and politics is from Goldsmiths College, the University of London. For more than two decades, he had taught qualitative research methodology in general, and ethnographic research in particular, for MPhil and PhD students. He is the author and editor of more than 30 books written in Chinese on collective memory, cultural identity and social changes.

MANTRA
BOOKS

EASTERN RELIGION & PHILOSOPHY

We publish books on Eastern religions and philosophies. Books that aim to inform and explore the various traditions that began in the East and have migrated West.

If you have enjoyed this book, why not tell other readers by posting a review on your preferred book site.

Recent bestsellers from MANTRA BOOKS are:

The Way Things Are
A Living Approach to Buddhism
Lama Ole Nydahl
An introduction to the teachings of the Buddha, and how to make use of these teachings in everyday life.
Paperback: 978-1-84694-042-2 ebook: 978-1-78099-845-9

Back to the Truth
5000 Years of Advaita
Dennis Waite
A demystifying guide to Advaita for both those new to, and those familiar with this ancient, non-dualist philosophy from India.
Paperback: 978-1-90504-761-1 ebook: 978-184694-624-0

Shinto: A celebration of Life
Aidan Rankin
Introducing a gentle but powerful spiritual pathway reconnecting humanity with Great Nature and affirming all aspects of life.
Paperback: 978-1-84694-438-3 ebook: 978-1-84694-738-4

In the Light of Meditation
Mike George
A comprehensive introduction to the practice of meditation and the spiritual principles behind it. A 10 lesson meditation programme with CD and internet support.
Paperback: 978-1-90381-661-5

A Path of Joy
Popping into Freedom
Paramananda Ishaya
A simple and joyful path to spiritual enlightenment.
Paperback: 978-1-78279-323-6 ebook: 978-1-78279-322-9

The Less Dust the More Trust

Participating in The Shamatha Project, Meditation and Science

Adeline van Waning, MD PhD

The inside-story of a woman participating in frontline meditation research, exploring the interfaces of mind-practice, science and psychology.

Paperback: 978-1-78099-948-7 ebook: 978-1-78279-657-2

I Know How To Live, I Know How To Die

The Teachings of Dadi Janki: A warm, radical, and life-affirming view of who we are, where we come from, and what time is calling us to do

Neville Hodgkinson

Life and death are explored in the context of frontier science and deep soul awareness.

Paperback: 978-1-78535-013-9 ebook: 978-1-78535-014-6

Living Jainism

An Ethical Science

Aidan Rankin, Kanti V. Mardia

A radical new perspective on science rooted in intuitive awareness and deductive reasoning.

Paperback: 978-1-78099-912-8 ebook: 978-1-78099-911-1

Ordinary Women, Extraordinary Wisdom

The Feminine Face of Awakening

Rita Marie Robinson

A collection of intimate conversations with female spiritual teachers who live like ordinary women, but are engaged with their true natures.

Paperback: 978-1-84694-068-2 ebook: 978-1-78099-908-1

The Way of Nothing
Nothing in the Way
Paramananda Ishaya
A fresh and light-hearted exploration of the amazing reality of nothingness.
Paperback: 978-1-78279-307-6 ebook: 978-1-78099-840-4

The Way of Nothing

Nothing in the Way

Paramananda Ishaya

A fresh and light-hearted exploration of the amazing reality of nothingness

Paperback: 978-1-78279-307-6 ebook: 978-1-78099-840-4

Readers of ebooks can buy or view any of these bestsellers by clicking on the live link in the title. Most titles are published in paperback and as an ebook. Paperbacks are available from traditional bookshops. Both print and ebook formats are available online.

Find more titles and sign up to our readers' newsletter at www.collectiveinkbooks.com/mind-body-spirit. Follow us on Facebook at facebook.com/OBooks and Twitter at twitter.com/obooks